TELLING STORIES TO TOUCH THE HEART

The audience sits before the teacher, braced for the onslaught of four biblical points, five easy steps, and two applications. At the same time heads are prepared to nod in agreement, the armor of lifelong habits stands ready to guard the heart from any possible pangs of conviction. Suddenly, without warning, the teacher begins to tell a story. Interest is built, holes open up in the armor, and truth shoots through like an arrow aimed at the heart. The teacher has succeeded. Why? Because he's just read *Telling Stories to Touch the Heart* by Reg Grant and John Reed.

Modern audiences have engaged Star Wars technology to guard their hearts from conviction. These two veteran motivational teachers have updated the age-old purveyor of truth—the well-told story—to effectively meet the challenge. This book is a secret weapon to be used with utmost care.

Howard G. Hendricks

TELLING STORIES TO TOUCH THE HEART

REG GRANT AND JOHN REED

VICTOR BOOKS®
A DIVISION OF SCRIPTURE PRESS PUBLICATIONS INC.
USA CANADA ENGLAND

Most Scripture quotations are from the *Holy Bible, New International Version,* © 1973, 1978, 1984, International Bible Society. Used by permission of Zondervan Bible Publishers. (Other quotations are from the *New American Standard Bible,* © the Lockman Foundation 1960, 1962, 1963, 1968, 1971, 1972, 1973, 1975, 1977.)

Library of Congress Cataloging-in-Publication Data

Grant, Reg, 1954–
    Telling stories to touch the heart / by Reg Grant and John Reed.
       p.   cm. — (Equipped for ministry series)
    Includes bibliographical references.
    ISBN 0-89693-820-4
    1. Storytelling in Christian education. 2. Homiletical
illustrations.   I. Reed, John (John W.), 1927–   . II. Title.
III. Series.
BV1534.3.G73   1990
268'.67 — dc20   90-36944
                                                               CIP

---

1 2 3 4 5 6 7 8 9 10 Printing/Year 94 93 92 91 90

CONTENTS

INTRODUCTION

Good things happen when you tell a story. You begin with, "It was the time of year when kings buckled on their armor, saddled their horses, and rode off to battle. . . ."

As you start, chattering slows to a tentative stop, movement freezes, and all eyes focus on you, the storyteller. You hook the imagination of your listeners with a sharply defined picture — kings, horses, armor. You enhance the image with movement — buckling, saddling, riding. You cross a threshold from this time back to an age of rattling swords, flashing spears, and the acrid smell of war. You construct your time machine of nouns and verbs that shimmer and echo in the mind; they magically transport your listeners not to the court of King Arthur, but to the palace roof of David, king of Israel. Your listeners are interested because they are involved. They are involved because you tickle their imagination with a story.

Stories have a way of sneaking past the defenses of the heart. Remember the story of Nathan and David in 2 Samuel 12? David had committed adultery with Bathsheba, then murdered her husband Uriah. David should have confessed his sin to God right away. Instead, he put it off. Maybe he rationalized, or tried to forget about it. Whatever David's defense, it was sufficient to insulate him from the spurs of conscience which should have prompted him to confess.

Finally, the Lord sent the Prophet Nathan to confront David with his sin. How did Nathan go about it? He told David a story. He involved David by asking him to pronounce judgment on a heartless rich man who had selfishly slain the pet lamb of a poor family. David was only too willing to judge the rich man for his lack of compassion. The man deserved to die, said David—after he had repaid four times over.

Nathan nailed him: "You are the man!" he said. David stood condemned by his own words. Until that time he had refused to confront his sin. Now, all his excuses came fluttering down around him like so many flimsy cards. There was no place left to hide. The pride of a king was broken. And it all began with a simple story.

The emphasis here is on "simple." Nathan didn't have a fancy stage or props or lights. He didn't have to change costumes in the middle of the story. There was no elaborate technique, no elevated language. He didn't have a lot of time; the whole story took less than one minute. And he had the smallest possible audience: just one man sharing a story with another. And yet that story changed the course of a life and a nation. But there was something else lacking here: there was no applause at the end.

Applause is often the expression of the casual observer, one who views the action of your story from a safe distance. He maintains objectivity because he wants to interpret the text honestly, not through the rose-colored glasses of emotion. Fear whispers in our rational left brain that if we allow ourselves to be drawn into a subjective experience of truth—that is, if we catch ourselves responding emotionally—we forfeit our ability to interpret that truth accurately. Emotions carry us into an interpretive fog, the argument goes; they dull the razor-sharp precision of objectivity.

But if the argument is true that we should attempt to remain bloodless in our scrutiny of a story, then why do the writers of Scripture relate most of God's truth in the form of stories? Why didn't Jesus simply slice away all the narrative from His parables as so much verbal fat, and leave us with lean (and tasteless) propositions? Why don't we stuff biblical truth into gelatin-coated pills that are quick and easy to swallow and guaranteed not to affect our appetite for the tasty stuff the world has to offer?

The answer: a well-told story touches the whole man, not just his intellect. You can ditch an annoying intellectual proposition without much effort, like flicking away a pesky mosquito. But try that with a story that has scraped your emotions raw. Try to ignore a parable that has battered your rebellious will into a defenseless pulp. King David couldn't ignore it. He couldn't rationalize it away because the story of the selfish rich man had touched him at every level: intellect, emotion, and will. He understood the problem, he responded passionately, and he decided the man deserved death.

As "the inheritors of Nathan's legacy,"[1] we need to realize that the intellect works in concert with the emotions and the will. These three parts of every human being work together either to promote the interests of God or to pursue the interests of the natural man. We are rather democratically composed, aren't we? It's as if the intellect, the emotions, and the will each have a vote. Our job as storytellers is to campaign for righteousness — to solicit the support of the intellect, the emotions, and the will in a concerted effort to vote against selfishness and in favor of righteousness. When we appeal to only one third of that which makes us human (the intellect), we leave two thirds (emotions and will) to argue the other side, to vote the other way. And if self-interest is the issue (as it always seems to be), the majority rules.

We fool and flatter ourselves if we think we can isolate our intellects to obtain absolute objectivity. We simply cannot make a decision, any decision, without emotion and will tugging at our intellectual sleeve. Will and emotion will annoy us to death if we try to ignore them — so let's put them to work for us. Let's engage them in the storytelling process and discover how much more effective our storytelling (and story-listening) can be!

A good story doesn't permit casual observation. It wraps you up in truth and recognition and won't let go. You are there, in the story; your imagination is kindled; you are involved; you interact with truth on a deep and personal level because you are in the story and now the story is in you. Then it's over, and you sit in the embrace of truth. The story is still resonating in the deepest part of you. For the moment, you are still because it simply takes some time to "get back." And once you emerge from the story, you are never the same again. That's what stories can do. That's why you want to be a storyteller.

Actually, you have been a teller of tales from the time you were a young child. Perhaps you were a far better storyteller then because your imagination was free from the static of life's disappointments. Storytelling is the most ancient of all arts and one of the most rewarding. Let us help you meet the exciting challenge of telling stories to touch the heart.

---

[1]William J. Bausch, *Storytelling: Imagination and Faith* (Mystic, Conn.: Twenty-Third Publications, 1984), 13.

ONE

"Before I Dive In..."

Who am I kidding? There's no way I can stand up in front of a group of people and tell a story without notes. Is there?

The ability to tell stories begins with a desire to tell stories. If you want to know how to tell a story to a group of people, then you can learn; it's that simple. The hard part isn't the learning—it's *deciding* to learn. If you are willing to take that first decisive step, then we can show you how to tell stories that will inform as well as transform your audience.

Let's start with a word of encouragement: you are already a storyteller! When you tell your spouse how your boss praised you at work, you are telling a story. When you and your buddies relive the three-pointer that saved the Lakers game, you are telling a story. When you call your best friend to tell her how your little Katy just won the lead in the school play, you are telling a story. The bargain you found at last Saturday's garage sale, your plans for moving, your family vacations, a hunting trip—you are telling stories all the time! Storytelling is so natural, so "daily," most of us would have to concentrate in order to not tell stories. So, what's to worry?

Observation:
What scares us isn't telling stories
(we do that all the time).
What scares us is telling *prepared* stories.

11

OK, how do I get over this fear?

You can begin to conquer the fear of telling prepared stories by reading stories or poems aloud rather than telling them from memory. You will be surprised at how fast your confidence grows as you learn to read with greater expression and variety.

I'm just a beginner. Where would I find someone to listen to me?

As for an audience, you may need to look no further than your own living room. Your family and friends know you and love you. You have a built-in support group right under your nose. So begin by reading stories to your mate, your kids, or your close friends.

Where should I start? What kind of story should I tell?

First, select one of your favorite poems or short stories. Better yet, find out what your audience likes (especially if you are reading to kids). Before you read it aloud, try it several times on your own to acquaint yourself with the words and phrasing.

Next, choose a partner. We suggest choosing a partner rather than an "audience" because the one who hears your story actually joins you in a partnership. When you tell a story, you aren't communicating *to* someone as much as *with* someone. That fortunate friend is not being acted upon as much as he or she is joining you in the adventure of the story. So, even though we speak of reading *to* your partner, we want to encourage the attitude of reading *with* him or her.

Robert Frost's "Stopping by Woods on a Snowy Evening" unveils a portrait of winter in a quiet wood. The author paused awhile in the midst of busyness to enjoy the slowness of the snow fashioning a landscape into a soft sculpture that would, in a moment, yield and crunch under his horse's hooves.

Stopping by Woods on a Snowy Evening

Whose woods these are I think I know.
His house is in the village though;
He will not see me stopping here
To watch his woods fill up with snow.

My little horse must think it queer
To stop without a farmhouse near

Between the woods and frozen lake
The darkest evening of the year.

He gives his harness bells a shake
To ask if there is some mistake.
The only other sound's the sweep
Of easy wind and downy flake.

The woods are lovely, dark and deep.
But I have promises to keep,
And miles to go before I sleep,
And miles to go before I sleep.[1]

Read Frost's poem to your partner, then talk about it—not only about what it means (though meaning is certainly important), but about how it makes you feel. It's important, especially in the beginning, to choose a partner with whom you feel free to express yourself honestly, without the constraints of worrying about what he or she will think or say. Explore the poem together.

What should we be looking for?

Look for the answers to questions such as, "Why does this poem make us laugh? Why does it make us want to slow down? The poem is bathed in a nostalgic longing for something that slips through the fingers as easily as moonlight on a winter night—why? What words does Frost use to draw us into the 'story' of the poem? Does 'Stopping by Woods on a Snowy Evening' leave you with a feeling that you need to *do* something? What is it, and why do you feel you must do it?"[2]

What's the benefit of this kind of analysis?

By following this personal discussion, you will discover that your next reading is infused with a new energy and depth. You will feel at ease in reading the story because you will understand it just a bit better for having explored it with a friend. It becomes *your* story, in a way, and by sharing it with others from your heart, it can become theirs as well. Stories build bridges between people. They are catalysts to conversation. They can rev up an old relationship or launch a new one.

What is the next step?

After you have read a few times to your close circle of friends

13

and family, broaden your audience to include your Sunday School class, your Bible study group, or the garden club. Their feedback, and the discussions your stories spark will only add fuel to your storytelling fire. You will find that "stage fright" begins to evaporate in the light of positive feedback.

Maybe it's my background, but I still feel inhibited. Did you ever struggle with feelings of inadequacy?

As a young man, John Reed suffered deep feelings of inferiority. The result: severe stage fright. Fear was with him day and night, crippling his ability to relate well with people. The confidence to be open and transparent in relationships simply wasn't there. It had been scared away.

Then he began to read to people. He had a college roommate who asked him to read "The Cremation of Sam Magee" by Robert W. Service to some of his buddies. John decided to take the chance. It was a turning point. His friends enjoyed the poem and told him so.

Then others began asking for the young man who could make a story come alive, the one who could read so well. Stage fright took a backseat. John found that speaking someone else's words, relating someone else's story, actually helped him relax and be himself in front of an audience.

All the energy that had for so long been wasted on fear was transformed. The fear that had haunted John actually became a friend. The Lord turned that destructive force into constructive energy that lent a vibrancy to his readings.

If you have stage fright, take courage. Read! Read to anyone who will listen. Read and keep on reading, because the more you read, the more you will enjoy storytelling and the better you will become.

All right, let's say I can muster the courage to read a story—a short one. After all, I'm starting from scratch. How do I read out loud to make a story interesting?

Make this a rule at the start: pray first that the Lord will start you on the path toward becoming an effective storyteller by making you an effective reader. Next, read the story through aloud several times on your own. You will find that the more often you read it to yourself, the more confident you will become and the better you will be able to read in public.

What do you mean by "several times?" Let's get specific!

Some find that reading the story aloud 20 to 30 times private-
ly allows them to be truly comfortable when they read to an
audience. Perhaps that would work for you as well. When reading a short story or poem, becoming comfortable with it really
doesn't take that long. Slip some "stand-up" reading time in
between other tasks during the day. You'll be surprised at how
quickly your rehearsals add up.

As you practice reading aloud to yourself, you might want to
mark the first few words of the major divisions of the story with
a highlighting pen. The reason is simple: when you read to a
group, you will want to focus your attention (your eyes and your
energy) on your audience rather than on the page. Highlighting
provides a visual cue so that when you look down to "grab" the
text with your eyes, you will readily see the major divisions of
thought colorfully marked off. You waste less time trying to find
your place since your eyes will be drawn directly to the highlighted part.

You only need to highlight the first few words of the major
divisions in the story—just enough to provide a flag for your
eyes. The highlight tells you, "There is a shift here." The
change may be one of mood or location or time. The point is
that the highlight provides a visual reminder of a change of
some kind in the story—a change that you will want to mirror
in your reading. If you were reading Joshua 1:8-9, you might
want to highlight your text like this:

> **Do not let** this Book of the Law depart from your
> mouth; meditate on it day and night, so that you may
> be careful to do everything written in it. Then you
> will be prosperous and successful.
> **Have I not** commanded you? Be strong and coura-
> geous. Do not be terrified; do not be discouraged, for
> the Lord your God will be with you wherever you go.

In this case, the first words of the two verses are highlighted
because there is a slight shift in thought between the verses
which allows for a tiny break. Determine where to highlight
based on the author's flow of thought. Remember, you won't
need to highlight for every time you look down. Only highlight
the major divisions of thought. You are speaking thoughts, not

just words, to people. You want to maintain eye contact with your audience as much as possible during the communication of that thought. Give it a try. You will be amazed at how confident you will become with a little practice.

Observation:
By the time you have orally rehearsed a selection 20–30 times, you will have it virtually memorized.
That translates into significantly less time spent with your eyes glued to the page.

How should I start the reading?
As you rehearse your reading, try these hints to help you get off to a clean start. Confidently stride to the rehearsal platform, carrying the closed book close to the body. Make sure your passage is marked, so that you don't have to fumble with finding the place in the book once you're in place on the platform. You can use your finger to mark the place, a ribbon marker if you are using a Bible, or a bookmark. How you mark it isn't the point. What's important is that you be able to open the book to the place once you are ready. Otherwise, you draw unnecessary attention to the mechanics of opening the text and finding your place.

That seems kind of nitpicky. Will anyone really notice?
Remember, it's the small things that count in a public reading. Every word you speak, every movement you make, says something to your audience. That "something" will either add salt to or throw sand on your story. Watch the details and notice how they are put together.

Audiences respond best to structured presentations. That's good for us because every story or poem you present will have a beginning, a middle, and an end. You can provide structural clues to help your audience relax and enjoy the story. Simply by letting them know where you are. Your clues can be verbal or nonverbal.

For example?
Before you begin to speak in your practice session, look your imaginary audience in the eye and smile. This signals that you are ready to begin and it's time to focus attention on you. You haven't spoken yet—you are simply gaining attention through

your physical presence and eye contact. You will then do one of two things: either begin your introduction, in which case you may prefer to leave your book closed; or launch right into the story without a formal introduction—open the book then.

Let's assume you are going to begin with an introduction. Since you will want your introduction to be as polished as your reading of the story, you will want to write it out and rehearse it just as you rehearse your reading. Your introduction should be brief and should set the mood and the context for your story. The objective is to corral your listeners' attention until the story ends. The first line of your introduction needs to be short, vivid, and appealing to the senses. For example:

> Smell
> "Holiness—it's the aroma of fresh-baked bread cooling on a windowsill."
>
> Hearing
> "The clank of hammer on nail split the morning air."
>
> Taste
> "It's the morning after the night before, and your mouth tastes like steel wool."
>
> Touch
> "Loneliness can cling to your heart like a wet sheet on a cold night."
>
> Sight
> "Once there was a man who could only see in black and white."

Why is the first line I speak so important?

Telling a story is a bit like going fishing. You wouldn't think of casting your line into the river without bait and a hook on it. The fish would stare at it for a moment, become bored, and swim off in search of more interesting food. Your listeners aren't that much different from a school of walleye. They want the first line you cast out to be attractive and tasty; then they will bite. And once they bite, they're hooked. Work hard on the first line. The entire introduction will probably be less than 30 seconds long (3–5 sentences). Here is an introduction John uses for a reading of 1 Samuel 1:

I love the joy of sunshine bursting through after the violence of a summer storm. Hannah's story is like that. As I read, watch the storms break over her life. See faith shine through.

Now that I have completed my introduction, what next?
Open your book. Don't look down to see where your place is yet — your eyes are still on your audience.

Can I leave the book on the lectern so I can use my hands?
We suggest holding your book, for a couple reasons. First, if the book is left on the lectern, your head will be bobbing up and down as you look down to read and then look up to speak. Holding the text allows you to glance down with your eyes using little, if any, distracting head movement. The second reason we suggest holding the text is that in the reading of a story, the book is the authority source, not the reader. This is one of the differences between reading a story out of a book (especially the Bible) and telling a story from memory. If you are holding the book, you are holding what the audience perceives to be the authority source. Your presentation is strengthened simply be-

cause you are physically connected to the source of the story.

Hold the book high enough so that, when you look down at the page, your head does not bob up and down. You should be able to glance down with your eyes, without much head movement. The book should be just high enough and far enough in front of you so that you can still see the people in the front row. Remember — if you can't see their faces, they can't see yours.

Hold the book with your left hand under the spine. Use your right hand to follow the words down the page. You will find that after practicing 20–30 times (if possible), your hand will go on "autopilot" and be at the right place at the right time. Then, when you glance down to see the first few words of the next thought, both your hand and the highlighted words will assist you in finding your place.

Is there a rule about how much I should look at the audience, and how much I should look at the page?

The ideal in reading is never to read any words aloud while looking down at the page. The times you glance down should correspond to natural breaks which fit into the flow of the narrative. When you speak, your eyes should either be on the audience or on the image you are creating for them (more about that later).

When you break eye contact with the audience, even for an instant, you introduce a momentary pause. Not all pauses are bad. In fact, they are a normal part of all communication. So don't fight them. Instead, use and enjoy pauses. You can look down after a phrase, during those natural breaks which punctuate (rather than interrupt) the flow of thought. The text itself will give you t he clues you need. Let's say you are working on Psalm 3. The text gives you clues as to the best places to look down.

> Psalm 3
> A psalm of David. When he fled from his son Absalom.
>
> ¹O Lord, how many are my foes! How many rise up against me!
> ²Many are saying of me, "God will not deliver him." *Selah*
> ³But You are a shield around me, O Lord; You bestow glory on me and lift up my head.
> ⁴To the Lord I cry aloud, and He answers me from His holy hill. *Selah*
> ⁵I lie down and sleep; I wake again, because the Lord sustains me.
> ⁶I will not fear the tens of thousands drawn up against me on every side.
> ⁷Arise, O Lord! Deliver me, O my God! Strike all my enemies on the jaw; break the teeth of the wicked.
> ⁸From the Lord comes deliverance. May your blessing be on your people. *Selah*

Note the three *selahs* at the end of verses 2, 4, and 8. *Selah* suggests the idea of a musical "rest" or "pause" to prepare for a shift in mood. There is your cue! The first section (vv. 1-2) focuses on desperation. The second section (vv. 3-4) shifts the focus away from the situation and onto what David knows to be true of the Lord. The third section (vv. 5-8) reveals David's confidence in God's delivering power. Three sections — each one marked off by a *selah*, or pause.

Of course, you are free to look down more than three times, breaking the phrases as you would in natural conversation. These *selahs* simply suggest specific places for three of the more definite pauses.

Here is how the reading would work, step by step. Glance down at the beginning of the psalm to see the highlighted words, **"O Lord, how many . . ."** Now look at the audience as you speak the first sentence to them. Glance down and "grab" the first words of the next sentence, "How many . . ." Look at the audience and deliver the line to them. Follow the same pattern, glancing down to get the first two or three words of each sentence, and then looking up to speak them to the audience. Just be sure you look down and give a more definite pause after each of the *selahs* in verses 2, 4, and 8. That's all there is to it! It just takes practice.

How can I help my listeners see what I'm describing to them?

You must see it first! Envision all the action of the story taking place in images that your mind's eye sees through an imaginary window just above the heads in the back row of the audience. The window is something like a large, wrap-around screen such as you may have seen at Disney World. If you drew two lines from yourself on the platform to the outside edges of your imaginary window, you should find yourself at the vortex of a 45-degree angle. Imagine you are seeing the action taking place through this imaginary window as you are reading.

Once your listeners see you "imaging" the action of the story, they will instinctively "sees" it on the "screen" of their minds. This intuitive ability to see pictures in our minds is one of God's gracious gifts to us.

Won't people be distracted by my looking over their heads?

Children may turn at first to see the image you are seeing over their heads, but it won't take them long to catch on and enjoy the experience. They will soon join you by seeing the story in their imaginations. The more detail you can fill in with your vivid imagination, the easier it will be for you to concentrate on the image. Then it will be easier for your audience to "see" what you are "seeing."

When you see a tree, for instance, see a specific tree: an oak or a poplar or a willow. When you see a giant, see all his armor, the flash of the sunlight on his spear, and the ugly wart on the end of his nose. It's all in your field of vision. But focus on only one part at a time, just as you would if you were actually looking at a giant. In your rehearsals, practice seeing everything there is to see in the scene. Then decide on and focus on the most important part of the scene. Remember too that in performance you will only look at the scene long enough to fix it on the imagination of the audience. As soon as possible, reestablish eye contact with them.

Let's take a specific story. How can I help them see it?

Suppose you want to recreate the little rock-throwing incident recorded in 1 Samuel 17. Here's one way to do it. Imagine you are a radio announcer whose job it is to broadcast the "play by play" of David's clash with Goliath. Your audience doesn't have TV. It's up to you, but you can do it. You can help them see the fight through your description. You can recreate for them the tension and some of the danger of that turning point in history.

Where should I imagine the important characters as I speak?

Place the armies of Israel over on the left-hand side (that is, your left as you face the audience) through the imaginary wrap-around window. The Philistine bad guys are clustered on the right-hand side. The huge gap in the middle is the Valley of Elah, where the showdown is about to take place. You watch Goliath strut out from the Philistine camp on the right side; he marches down to the center of the valley (which also happens to be the center of your window). He taunts Israel from that spot until a kid emerges from the cowering ranks on the left-hand side of the screen. Your eyes follow the teenager as he walks confidently from your left down to the center of the valley. It's high noon, the buzzards are circling overhead — and you see it all. What's fascinating is that, as you see it, you will be able to sense that your audience, your partners in this adventure, can see it too!

Will I notice some kind of response in the audience if they are seeing what I'm seeing?

Good imaging can galvanize an impression on the heart of your audience. You will notice a stillness in the room. A hush descends like a blanket and the audience is with you in the story. Congratulations! You have accomplished in just a few minutes what mindless hours in front of a television have failed to do. You have sparked the collective imagination of a group of people — a group of people who may share only one thing in common — a desire to hear you tell a story.

Imaging allows you to reveal the life that is in the story or poem. When you practice imaging in your Bible reading, you may hear people say later, "I *saw* Paul in prison writing to the Ephesians. I could almost *feel* the dampness of that cold floor. It seems so real to me now." Consistent imaging yields great rewards, but it calls for great concentration. You can do it with practice.

Observation:
If you see the action of the story,
so will your listeners.
If you don't see it,
they won't either.

23

When the characters in your story speak to one another — that is, anytime you are "inside quotations marks" — always imagine the characters near the center of your screen. This can be the place of conversation between all the characters in your story, regardless of where the action happens on the imaginary screen.

Let's say, for example, that Moses and Aaron are preparing to cross the Red Sea on the left side of the window. That's where the "action" of the scene is going on. Now Moses and Aaron are going to speak to one another. Rather than keeping them scroonched together with three million other Israelites on the left side of the image, place them with your imagination directly in the middle of the window. This repositioning works because, when you move them to the center, it is as if you "zoom in" on just those two individuals to hear what they are saying. Putting them in the center isolates them from the crowd and helps focus attention on what is being said. When the dialogue is complete and the action resumes, then you redirect the focus to the left side of window image.

When one character speaks to another, you as the reader should always "look" at the person being addressed. Always place the people to whom you speak on the imaginary screen before you. Resist the temptation to bring characters "on stage" with you. Keep them out front on the screen above the heads of your audience. For example, if Moses is speaking to Aaron, and you are reading Moses' lines, then imagine you are really seeing Aaron standing there near the center of your imaginary window and speak directly to him. In a sense, you are then playing the part of Moses.

You now know when to look at the image. But eye contact with your listeners is important too. So when should you look at them?

The rule is: "The audience is more important than the image." You want to look at your audience as much as possible. There are no absolute rules that tell you when to look at your image and when to look at your audience, but you may find these general suggestions helpful. You will want to look at your audience during your introduction. This is the first impression you will make, and you want it to be a strong one. Look at the audience too when you want to associate them favorably with a group of people in the reading. For example, when Paul is praising the Colossians for their faith and love in Colossians 1:4, pretend that your audience is the Colossian congregation. Look right into their eyes and speak to them just as Paul would have. It simply and subtly reinforces the love that you have for your people.

Look at your listeners as well during long narrative sections when there isn't a great deal of action. Look at them during scene descriptions after you have placed the elements of the scene on the screen. Look at them even during some parts of the dialogue, especially if the dialogue is extended.

By the way, remember to look at individuals in the audience rather than at clusters of people. Really see them. Some storytellers never actually *see* the audience at all, even though they are looking right at them. You should not look at one person for more than four or five seconds before moving to another. When your eyes meet the eyes of another person and you see one another, if only for a few seconds, the effect can be startling in its impact. You have made contact. You are communicating.

Here are a few suggestions for when you want to look at the image you are creating for the audience. Look at the image of your characters when they are talking to each other. This is the "character image." Look at the image of the scene you have created on the imaginary screen when there is a wonderful vision being described in the story (Ezekiel 1, for example, or Isaiah 6). This is the "scene image."

Your image may have several parts. This is where the idea of the wrap-around screen is especially helpful. It allows you to see in considerable detail the various elements of the story.

Look at the scene image when there is an evil person or crowd of people that you do not want to associate with your listeners by looking directly at them. For example, do not look at a woman in your audience when you are describing Jezebel or the Wicked Witch of the West. You can make enemies just as quickly as you can make friends.

How you feel toward your audience can make a profound difference in the effectiveness of your story. Read as if you are reading to your child, your grandchild, or a friend, but not a group; that is, read personally, speaking in your natural voice. One of the great temptations when reading to children is to take on a "baby voice," a saccharin-sweet phrasing that leaves the children feeling sticky after the story. Use your natural voice, especially with children; they can spot a phony a mile away.

Let's talk about pacing, the rate at which you read your story. Take your time; don't rush the words. Give your audience time to see the images and hear the sounds the words conjure up. You must take time to see the image in your mind just before you say the words; that will help the audience see it with you. The order, then, is: glance down at the story, look up, see the image, and describe it.

The same rule applies to "hearing" a sound or voice in the story. "Hear" it first, then respond. Of course, there will be a brief pause as you "hear" the sound, or "see" the image, but it will work for you because the pause is filled with action. The flow of the story is maintained. Pauses are great as long as they are pauses of substance. What you want to avoid is a void—a pause that is nothing but a mindless black hole.

When you are reading a prayer or a quotation that is specifically addressed to God, you may not feel comfortable looking at your audience. You might try looking at a spot located at the center of the top of the back wall, just where it reaches the ceiling. If you are reading in an auditorium with a balcony, you might be comfortable looking at a spot on the center of the balcony facing.

How do I close? How do I get off the stage?

If the text will allow it, slow the pace of the last paragraph. Coast, do not screech, to a stop. Close the book. Look at your audience as you pause for a brief moment. Then confidently return to your seat, carrying your book close to the body.

There! That wasn't so hard, was it? Here's some good news: you have already learned many of the rules for telling a story from memory. You're halfway home and going strong! Let's keep moving!

----

[1] From *The Poetry of Robert Frost* edited by Edward Connery Latham. Copyright 1923, © 1969 by Holt, Rinehart and Winston. Copyright 1951 by Robert Frost. Reprinted by permission of Henry Holt and Company, Inc.

[2] Be careful about reading too much into "Stopping by Woods on a Snowy Evening." Mr. Frost's daughter, Leslie, told John Reed that her father "simply saw a beautiful wood in the snow and wrote about it. Nothing 'deeper' was intended."

TWO

"Just One More Question ...Well, Maybe Two!"

My confidence is up, but I don't quite feel ready for the big plunge into telling a prepared story from memory. Is there a transition between reading and telling?

Try telling familiar stories out of your own experience. You have any number of topics to choose from. You may wish to begin by telling your children or your spouse the most spine-tingling adventure you have ever had. Make sure the story has a beginning, middle, and end. Include only those details which are important to the development of the story. Don't let any unimportant details distract you, or you will find yourself wandering in one of Bunyan's "By-path Meadows" with no signs to guide you back to the main path of the story.

Decide which details are necessary to the progress of your adventure. Then flesh out those details, using verbs that resonate and nouns that have meat on them. Avoid verbs such as "is" and "are," followed by adjectives and adverbs.

Compare, for instance, "Her words were painful" with "She speaks poniards [daggers], and every word stabs."[1]

Try to stay in the active voice and avoid the passive (using action verbs will help here). What if our more literate forefathers had stumbled over the active voice? We may have inherited something like this:

"Let liberty be given to me, or death be given to me!"

"Let the Alamo be remembered!"

"You are wanted by Uncle Sam!"

You are probably ready now to tell a story to your Sunday School class. Let's start with how you came to faith in Christ. The pitfall to watch out for here is Christian jargon — stained-glass phrases designed to showcase a saint. The sad effect of such condescending prattle is to cast a shadow of benign "holier-than-thouness." Just relax, be yourself, and have fun sharing the best news in the world. Let your language be vivid, but natural; seasoned with salt, but according to your recipe.

How long should these personal stories be?

Don't satiate your listeners — leave them hungry. Always finish your story but keep a close eye on the clock. If the occasion or event allows you 15 minutes to tell a story or give a message, plan to end after 14 minutes and 30 seconds. We have yet to hear one person out of the thousands to whom we have spoken complain about getting to go home early. Don't gain a reputation for being long-winded! Of course, if you are telling a story in your home to your family, the time restrictions are less pressing. But your home is the best environment in which you can begin to practice careful time management. Your audience will appreciate your professionalism and you will be a more precise (not to mention more considerate) storyteller as a result.

Should I always use personal stories when I teach?

The number of stories you can tell out of your own experience depends on how good your memory is, how observant you are, and how long you have lived. Therefore, given enough time, your reservoir of stories would eventually run dry. But there is a deeper well to draw from. Our Lord has given you a wellspring of imagination which can supply a practically endless stream of story plots, characters, and locations. The more you exercise your imaginative muscle in creative storytelling, the more you will find yourself discovering new angles, new perspectives, and fresh applications on timeless truths.

How can I develop my imaginative muscle?

You can develop your imagination by simply becoming more observant of the world around you. The next time you are out on a starlit night, take some time to really look at the stars. Pick out one star and ask yourself, "What is it like?" Careful now. Try to avoid the technical jargon of the astrophysicist. To the mind's eye, a star must be more than "any self-luminous celestial body, exclusive of comets, meteors, and nebulae." It may look like a single sparkling marble, or like a jewel in a black crown, or like a firecracker that has just popped. Any one of these similes suggests a story.

Do you find one kind of audience to be better than another for a beginning storyteller?

The most natural audience in the world for your "make-believe" stories is children — uninhibited, honest, and wonderfully receptive to a good tale. Their hearts possess a particular quality that time seems to dilute as they grow up: the quality of immediate immersion. Children can immerse themselves in a story at the drop of a "Once upon a time. . . ." They possess the enviable ability of absolute abandonment to the desire of knowing "what happened next?!" Theirs is the joy of discovering uncharted seas; of slicing through the fog of a cloud-encased island where dreams come true. In the lap of the storyteller, children discover the thrill and the wonder of pretending and learning all rolled into one joyful experience called "story."

The joy of discovery isn't restricted to kids. You can discover along with them as you make these stories up on the spot. One fun way to do this is to ask one of the children to pick out an object in the room. Then you improvise a story around that object. You will be amazed at your own creative abilities as you weave a golden adventure out of the straw of ordinary stuff: a diaper becomes a magic carpet for talking mice; a pencil is transformed into a rocket ship for the tiny inhabitants of the doomed city of Rug; a bed turns into a flying bunk that can take you to the moon and back in just five minutes; Mars is red because it is covered with cherry trees that grow out of red sand. You can teach great truths with these highly imaginative "bedtime" stories. By the way, don't save them for bedtime. Tell them to your tribe whenever the mood hits you and the harvest is ripe. Once you are comfortable telling stories in your home, addressing a group will be a cinch.

How do I decide what kind of story my group needs?

The first rule in deciding what kind of story should be told is to know your audience. The effect of your first foray into storytelling may startle you, especially if you don't understand the needs of your audience. Stories are change agents. They will almost invariably excite a response, though it may not be the one you anticipate. Remember the story the Amalekite told

King David regarding the death of Saul in 2 Samuel 1? He lied to David, claiming he had killed Saul, though we know from 1 Samuel 31 that Saul killed himself. Perhaps he hoped to receive a reward for having brought the "good" news of Saul's death. His story got a response, but not the one he had hoped for; David had him executed on the spot for claiming to have slain the King of Israel.

Is choosing the right story really that important?

Choosing the wrong story may not get you killed, but it could wound your reputation. Choose your stories carefully, and they will serve you well.

Every storyteller in the Bible shares at least one thing in common: each tells in order to teach. There are lessons to learn, and often stories are the best way to get the point across. The story will entertain, but entertainment is never its primary goal. Your goal as a storyteller is to present the truth in such a captivating way that the hearer will be moved to action. We desire in our stories not merely to inform an intellect but to transform a life. To that end, we must find out what our listeners' needs are. Find out where their interests lie. Unlock the door to their needs with the key of an interesting story.

How do I find out what those needs are?

You can ask three questions to help discover the needs of a specific audience. Since these questions help us focus on the needs of a specific audience, we will call them focusing questions.[2]

The first focusing question is, "Does my story need to explain something (terms, setting, relationships)?" Your audience may not understand key ideas, such as reconciliation, propitiation, redemption, the church, or salvation. Your job as a storyteller is to wrap these abstract theological concepts up inside a person, animal, or object. Then tell a story that illustrates the meaning of that idea. You will often find yourself moving from the abstract to the concrete in order to help your audience see what you are talking about. If you are creating a story from scratch, you may want to ask yourself, "What is this abstract idea like?" in order to discover a central figure around which you can construct a story.

How about an example?

You may think of sin as a rabid black panther who hasn't

eaten in two weeks. Not only does the picture arrest attention, but it accurately reflects sin as presented in Genesis 4:7, "Sin is crouching at your door; and it desires to have you." Then build your story around your central image of a devouring beast. Your audience won't want to have anything to do with sin. Remember, you will strengthen your story if you can find your metaphor in the pages of the Bible itself.

As you continue to address the first focusing question, you can ask yourself: "Does this idea appeal to one of my senses?" The panther not only appeals to the eye, but to the ear (since we can hear it scream in the night) and to our sense of fear. Your abstract idea may ignite other senses as well.

Let's take another example of an abstract theological term: "holiness." Once you have studied the word as it is used in Scripture, you find that it means "the quality of being set apart, usually for a specific purpose." Yes, your definition is accurate, but it still doesn't help communicate the idea because it is still too clinical, too abstract, and too general.

So ask yourself, "To what do my senses respond that is 'set apart, usually for a specific purpose'"? How about fresh-baked bread? It appeals to your sense of smell and taste. There's only one appropriate response to a warm loaf of fresh-baked bread! If you created a brief story using this image, it might look something like this.

> The drive into school had become monotonous—day after day, the same route, the same routine. At the time, all I had to think about was this word study I had been doing on holiness—it didn't help. But there was always a brief interlude during my drive time. It always lifted my spirits just a bit, it nearly always made me smile, and it happened at the same spot every day. As I approached the corner of Mockingbird and Central, I would begin to prepare myself. Ready? Now breathe! Ahh, the aroma of fresh-baked bread slipped out of the corner bakery and into my car like an old friend. It was warm and wholesome and could take the chill off the day—and off my attitude. That bread had been baked and set aside for one thing.

That's a pretty good description of what the Bible calls holiness. Something is holy if it is set aside for a special purpose — like baked bread. Though I hadn't consciously considered it in those terms, I must have always thought of holiness as dry toast rather than fresh-baked bread. Our Lord Jesus was holy, and He was anything but dry and boring. How did He describe Himself in John 6:35 and 48? He is the "bread of life." We are to partake of Him. That's really the only appropriate response to Him, isn't it? I hadn't seen it before, but holiness is attractive after all.

Observation:

A carefully chosen metaphor which appeals to the senses can add immeasurably to your audience's understanding of abstract (though important) ideas.

What if my audience understands the basic concepts involved?

In that case, consider the second focusing question: "Does my story need to prove a point?" This question acknowledges that your audience doesn't necessarily buy what you are trying to sell. They may find it difficult, for example, to accept a particular teaching of Scripture (a wife's submission to her husband, mutual submission between husband and wife, our need to obey the government even in the "little" things). Rather than explaining, you need to convince them of the validity of what they may consider to be a controversial interpretation or application.

Observation:
It usually isn't the interpretation
the listeners balk at;
it is more often the implications
of that interpretation —
what they will have to do,
how they will have to change if you are right!

This kind of story will also inform, won't it?

Yes, but the emphasis will be on persuasion. Your goal is to convince the audience that Scripture does clearly reveal God's will in these cases, and that His will is reasonable; that is, it is designed for His glory and our ultimate good. This second focusing question is the one you will most often need to answer. Of course, your approach in the story should be sensitive and edifying. Stories are powerful; they can turn friends into enemies as easily as they can turn enemies into friends. Remember David and the Amalekite!

The third focusing question addresses a need to apply a truth that is already understood and accepted: "Do I need to emphasize how the lesson my story teaches applies to life?" Your audience may not immediately see the relevance of a particular lesson or may misinterpret it. A story can change that by focusing attention on the wonderful difference this lesson can make in the life of a believer if he or she will act on that knowledge.

For example, let's say you are ministering to a group of singles. You are trying to find a story that illustrates the subtle allure of lust and what is needed to overcome it. As you rummage through your illustration file, you may spark a memory of something you have read or heard when you ask yourself, "What is lust like? Have I read or heard anything that portrayed lust in terms of a simile ('lust is like sweet poison') or metaphor ('love is sweet poison') that would help my audience see it as it is?" Then you run across a card in your topical file. The card is labeled, "Lust, effects of" and underneath the heading you read, "See C.S. Lewis, *The Great Divorce*, chapter 11." (Ah, the glory of a good filing system.)

You find your volume, and in chapter 11 read that Lewis depicted lust as a perverse lizard perched on the shoulder of the one he tormented day and night. The degrading effects of the man's prolonged submission to the demands of lust seep from every simpering pore. Lewis goes on to reveal how lust can be vanquished, and how life can be transformed once lust is killed. When the lizard (the symbol of lust) is destroyed, it is transformed into a glorious white stallion. The man mounts and rides off to the heavenly mountains. After the wonderful metamorphosis, the Teacher of the story brings home the lesson to his student:

"Do ye understand all this, my Son?" said the Teacher.

"I don't know about *all*, Sir," said I. "Am I right in thinking the Lizard really turned into the Horse?"

"Aye. But it was killed first. Ye'll not forget that part of the story?"

"I'll try not to, Sir. But does it mean that every-thing—everything—that is in us can go on to the Mountains?"

"Nothing, not even the best and noblest, can go on as it now is. Nothing, not even what is lowest and most bestial, will not be raised up again if it submits to death. It is sown a natural body, it is raised a spiritual body. Flesh and blood cannot come to the Mountains. Not because they are too rank, but be-cause they are too weak. What is a Lizard compared with a stallion? Lust is a poor, weak, whimpering, whispering thing compared with that richness and energy of desire which will arise when lust has been killed."[3]

An edited version of chapter 11 of *The Great Divorce* can provide a vivid portrayal of the menacing subtlety of lust and how it can be overcome. If you are careful to avoid caricatures, but pursue an honest portrayal of the characters in the story, then you will leave your audience with an abhorrence of lust and its attendant impurities, and with a longing for the joy that awaits us in what Lewis calls "pure desire."

Focusing questions are designed to help you assess the needs of your particular listeners. Once you understand what they need, you can create or choose an appropriate story. Then you can emphasize those elements in the story which will meet those needs precisely.

But there is always a risk: you are staking the effectiveness of the lesson on the effectiveness of the story, which is the convey-or of that lesson. The temptation for the dedicated Bible student is to sacrifice a wonder-filled story on the twin altars of pedantry and thoroughness. We teachers can be so overly concerned with unnecessary detail—so "schoolmarmish"—that the story shrivels like a raisin under the withering sun of our intellect.

Thoroughness presents another problem. We often feel compelled to pack our stories with all the truth there is on a given subject. It's a fine sentiment, but we cannot afford to yield to the temptation to "cram." Yes, we want to be thorough in our study of the lesson but, as I have heard Howard Hendricks say in the classroom, "we don't want to dump the whole load of hay on one heifer!" You can't include all there is to know (or even all that *you* know) about justification, for instance, in one story. Give people truth in bite-size chunks that are easily digestible. Show them how God's truth works in life through a good story, and you may even get them into the Word for themselves!

---

[1]Benedick in Shakespeare's *Much Ado About Nothing*, 2.1.255. Not that you want to speak Elizabethan English, but Shakespeare did have a feel for words that has endured the test of time.

[2]Haddon Robinson calls these questions the Developmental Questions in his book *Biblical Preaching* (Grand Rapids, Mich.: Baker Book House, 1980) pages 77–100.

[3]C.S. Lewis, *The Great Divorce* (Macmillan: New York, 1946). Copyright 1946 C.S. Lewis. Published in the United Kingdom by Collins (London).

THREE

The First "R" of
Storytelling: Reading

I'm no theologian. Where do I start in preparing a Bible story?

Begin by reading the story thoroughly and taking a few notes. This is one of the most exciting steps in the storytelling process because here you get to wear the explorer's hat. You are the discoverer, the great finder, the unveiler of treasures. You aren't scratching in the dust for some dried-out, shriveled-up truth. No, you are on a treasure hunt. There's one remarkable thing about treasure: it's just as valuable (sometimes more so) and just as useful when you find it as when it was buried. On the pages of Scripture lie jewels with a unique property: they make you richer as you give them away.

Read slowly; take your time. You don't find gold by racing through the mine. Read the same story in different versions. If you normally read in the *King James Version,* try a *New American Standard;* or *The Holy Bible, New International Version;* or Phillips' *New Testament in Modern English;* or *The Living Bible.* Sometimes a different translation will help clear up a verse that has been cloudy to you. Jot down your observations: anything in the story that interests you, questions you have, ideas that pop into your head that seem at the moment to be random. Write them down — you may see their significance later.

Remember, nothing is too small to record. Let God's Word wash through your mind as you pan for His gold. Most people do pretty well at the small stuff. We have seen first-year semi-

nary students find as many as 100 legitimate observations in
Acts 1:8! Believe it or not, what a lot of students miss is the big
picture. They can count the leaves, but they miss the tree. They
count the sprinkles and forget to eat the cookie. The discovery
is there, but the joy is missing.

One way to see the big picture is to ask the obvious questions — the questions no one else will ask when you are in a
group ("Everyone knows that"). The secret is that people would
like to know, only they are too afraid to ask. The odd thing is
that you don't have to be in a group to feel intimidated. It can
happen when you're all alone. Ever have a conversation like this
with yourself?

> ME: Who wrote Ecclesiastes?
> MY PRIDE: Oh, everyone knows that!
> ME: Afraid not, 'cause I don't know.
> MY PRIDE: How long did you say you've been a Chris-
> tian? Asking who wrote Ecclesiastes at your age?
> Honestly! You're still a baby, aren't you? Drinking
> milk when you ought to be enjoying steak. What
> possible difference could it make who wrote the
> book? Besides, you wouldn't know where to start
> looking! Let's get on to the really heady stuff so you
> can impress your Bible study group. You only have so
> much time, you know.

The way to handle the intimidator at this point is to keep one
thing in mind: reading time should not become bogged down in
your trying to find answers to hard questions. Nor is it the time to
interpret (unless a possible interpretation springs to mind while
you are exploring; even then, verify it later—keep moving).

The smart treasure hunter gathers his or her information first,
then takes it back to the lab for analysis. Imagine trying to
analyze all the data in the field. Frustration would dog your trail,
whining, "You'll never get all the work done—why even try?"
Keep exploring. You have five indispensable tools in your pack
to help you dig and sift: *who, when, where, why,* and *how.*

Time to Pull out the Tools, One by One
Tool #1: Who? When you ask "who?" you are looking for the

author, the original audience, the main characters, the supporting cast, and the "extras." Knowing the author and the readers will sometimes shed light on the text. Learning to distinguish the more important characters from the less important will help you in two ways. First, you will learn to highlight the more important characters; second, you will learn to avoid "majoring on a minor."

I often find interesting background material in Bible commentaries and histories. Would I be "adding to Scripture" by adding some of these details to my story? If not, how do I know how much to add and what to leave out?

When you tell the story from memory and you are dealing with minor characters, you may be tempted to spend a great deal of time describing the background of their positions or trades, the clothes they wear, or their facial expressions. This is not "adding to Scripture" since you do not claim that the words of your story are inspired by God. Besides, accurate details do not contradict the biblical record.

Though you won't be adding to Scripture, you may be drawing an inordinate amount of attention to a part of the story that neither advances the action nor prepares listeners for the lesson to be learned. We hope that the background information you add will enhance your audience's ability to enter into the story, rather than attract attention to itself.

The next time you are viewing one of your Rembrandts(!), notice that his use of light and shadow accomplishes two goals: the shadows downplay the peripheral visual information by muting colors and detail, while the light focuses our attention on the dominant image — the main character of the portrait, so to speak — where we discover great detail and colors that breathe life into the canvas.

Notice the way your vision functions in the natural world. Look at an object — a tree, let's say. See how the more you focus on the tree, the less detail you see in the grass, the sky, the fence, the house beside the tree. When you ask "who?" (or for that matter, "when?" "where?" "why?" and "how?"), all you are doing is finding out where the focus should be. Peripheral details in a story are important, but they are there to frame the central characters, not to distract our attention. Let's look at, for example, the story of David and Goliath in 1 Samuel 17.

Who wrote the story?
Answer: Not sure (we'll look this up later).

Who was the original audience?
Answer: Not sure.

Who are the "main characters" — those who will receive primary
focus or "star billing" in the story?
Answer: 1. David (for Israel)
         2. Goliath (for the bad guys)

Who would the "supporting cast" be — persons who should receive less attention than the main characters?
Answer: 1. Saul
         2. Eliab, Abinadab, and Shammah (the three oldest
             brothers of David)
         3. Jesse (David's father)

Who are the "extras" — the observers who will be affected by the
actions of the main characters but who add little to the story's
development?
Answer: 1. The army of the Philistines
         2. The army of Israel

Time to Pull the Second Tool from Your Pack
Tool #2: When?

When was this story written?
Answer: Not sure.

When did it take place?
Answer: During the reign of King Saul (not sure of the year).

Are there any other time references in the story?
Answer: 1. Jesse was old (1 Sam. 17:12).
         2. The three oldest sons of Jesse were fighting in
             Saul's army (17:13).
         3. David was the youngest of Jesse's sons (17:14).
         4. Goliath taunted Israel for forty days (17:16).
         5. David left to take food to his brothers early in
             the morning (17:20).
         6. He reached the camp when the army of Israel
             was going out to its battle positions (17:20).

7. When the Israelite army saw Goliath, they ran from him in great fear (17:24).
8. When David spoke with the other soldiers, his older brother Eliab accused him of acting wickedly (17:28).
9. David, a youth, was contrasted with Goliath, who had been fighting from his youth (17:33).
10. When a lion and bear threatened David's flock, he killed them (17:35).
11. When Goliath saw that David was a boy, he despised him (17:42).
12. David promised Goliath that on that day, the Lord would give Goliath into his hand (17:46).
13. When the Philistines saw that their hero was dead, they turned and ran away (17:51).

Take out the Third Tool and Keep Digging
Tool #3: Where?

Where did this battle take place?
Answer: Socoh in Judah; more specifically, the Philistines camped at Ephes Dammim, between Socoh and Azekah, while Saul and the Israelites assembled and camped in the Valley of Elah (17:1). Don't look these places up on a map—we'll do that later.

Does the author bring out other geographical details?
Answer: 1. Goliath was from Gath (17:4).
2. Goliath stood in the Valley of Elah as he challenged the army of Israel (17:3, 8).
3. David was from Bethlehem in Judah (17:12).
4. David traveled back and forth between the Israelite army and Bethlehem (17:15).
5. David tended his father's sheep in the desert (17:28).
6. Goliath's shield bearer always went in front of him (17:7, 41).
7. The Israelites, upon Goliath's death, pursued the Philistines to the entrance of Gath and to the gates of Ekron (17:52).
8. The Philistine dead were strewn along the Shaaraim road to Gath and Ekron (17:52).

9. David took Goliath's head to Jerusalem and put his weapons in his own tent (17:54).

Now We are Ready for the Fourth and Most Dangerous Tool
Tool #4: Why?

Note the warning label: "Handle with extreme caution." How very easy it is to read motives into the actions of characters when the text is silent on the matter. Most of the time, it is simply impossible to determine why a man or woman acted or thought in a particular way. The biblical evidence is too sketchy to draw definitive conclusions in most cases. If the text (and the larger context) doesn't reveal why a character behaved in a particular way, then it would be wise not to take a firm stand on the matter in your telling of the story. Regardless of how good your conclusion makes the story, the story won't last if it's built on quicksand. Build it instead on the rock-solid evidence of the text within its context.

Look for clues that suggest a purpose or reason for a particular action. Explanatory words such as "for," "in order to," "in order that," and "because" beckon you to look for purpose. For example, David used to go back and forth from Saul to Bethlehem. Why? What was his purpose in going? The text tells us he returned to Bethlehem to tend his father's sheep (17:15). The context suggests David often went to Saul's camp because he and his father Jesse were interested in his brothers' welfare (17:18, 22). Here are a few more purpose statements from 1 Samuel 17.

1. The Philistines gathered their armies "for battle" (17:1).
2. Saul grouped his army "to meet the Philistines" (17:2).
3. Goliath demanded that Israel give him a man in order that they may "fight each other" (17:10).
4. David ran to the battle line in order to greet his brothers (17:22).
5. Goliath came forward "to defy Israel" (17:25).
6. Eliab assumed that David "came down only to watch the battle" (17:28).
7. Saul told David he couldn't fight Goliath because he was "only a boy" while Goliath had "been a fighting man from his youth" (17:33).

8. Goliath was to be like the lion and the bear which David had killed "because he . . . defied the armies of the living God" (17:36).

9. David tried out Saul's armor and helmet first "because he was not used to them" (17:39).

10. The Philistine mocked David because "he was only a boy, ruddy and handsome" (17:42).

11. David boasted his confidence that God would give him victory over the Philistines in order that "the whole world will know that there is a God in Israel" (17:46).

12. David went out to battle with nothing but a stick and a sling so that "all those gathered . . . will know that it is not by sword or spear that the Lord saves; for the battle is the Lord's, and He will give all of you into our hands" (17:47).

Note that often as you answer the question "When?" you will find answers which also answer the question "Why?" For example, it is true that the Israelites ran from Goliath *after* they saw him ("when"); but in this case, it is more important to note that they ran *because* they saw a giant ("why").

Put on your detective's cap and pull out your magnifying glass. Often a closer look will yield greater insight: what initially seems an observation about the *time* of an event (a "when" type of observation) frequently becomes a recognition of *cause and effect* (a "why" type). Another example is 1 Samuel 17:11, "On hearing the Philistines's words, Saul and all the Israelites were dismayed and frightened." On the surface, this looks like a simple time reference. First Saul and Israel heard the giant, then they were afraid. But the more significant point is that the Israelites were afraid because of what the giant said and because of how he looked (vv. 4-7). This simple observation is a significant one, since it reveals how easily Israel was influenced by external appearances—a point you may want to emphasize in the telling (or reading) of the story.

Try the Last Tool in Your Pack
Tool #5: How?

In asking "How?" you look for longer descriptive passages which paint a picture in some detail. The author may want to emphasize how the main characters dress, or how they act or react in a specific situation. Any time you notice the author "zooming in for a close-up," looking in detail at what is felt or said or seen or heard or tasted or smelled, then it is time to ask, "How?"

How did Goliath dress?
Answer: 1. He wore a bronze helmet (17:5).
2. He was clothed with scale armor which weighed five thousand shekels of bronze (17:5).
3. He wore bronze greaves on his legs (17:6).
4. He had a bronze javelin slung between his shoulders (17:6).
5. He carried a huge spear whose shaft was like a weaver's rod and whose iron head weighed six hundred shekels — about 15 pounds (17:7).

How did David dress?
Answer: 1. He did not wear the bronze helmet and armor that Saul provided for him (17:39).
2. He took a stick (17:40).
3. He wore the clothing of a shepherd, which included a shepherd's bag (17:40).
4. He took five smooth stones (17:40).
5. He carried his sling in his hand (17:40).

How did Goliath address David?
Answer: Goliath boasted with self-confidence (17:42-44).

How did David address Goliath?
Answer: David expressed confidence in God (17:45-47).

How did the giant approach David?
Answer: He rose and came and drew near (17:48).

How did David approach the giant?
Answer: He ran quickly toward the battle line (17:48).

Now I know a bit about the details of the scene, but I still feel like the characters are lifeless. What's missing?

Emotion. So far you have used your five tools to dig up some interesting observations about the physical appearance of the main characters and the action of the story.

Now let's pull out our emotional Geiger counter. This tool helps identify the dominant emotions in the text. Sometimes the emotions are identified explicitly; sometimes they are implied. We need to be careful not to read into the text emotions that are not there, but we also need to be sensitive to clues the text gives us. Identifying these emotions will help us "get under the skin" of the characters we are talking about. The more real the characters and situations become to us, the more alive they will be to our audiences.

Does the text identify any emotions for us explicitly — emotions that are not hidden but are right out in the open?

Answer: 1. Saul and the armies of Israel were "dismayed" at the challenge of Goliath (17:11).

2. Saul and the armies of Israel were "terrified" of Goliath (17:11, 24).

3. Eliab "burned with anger" toward David for coming down to the battle line (17:28).

4. Goliath "despised" David when he saw that David was a boy (17:42).

Does the text identify any emotions for us implicitly — emotions that are hidden or undercover, not obvious?

Answer: 1. David must have felt confidence in the Lord when he volunteered to fight Goliath (17:32).

2. The armies of the Philistines must have been afraid of the God of Israel since they turned and ran after Goliath's death (17:51).

3. David, Saul, and the armies of Israel must have felt joy when David killed Goliath (17:52).

At this point, you have made a number of helpful observations, but you aren't finished yet. Keep your explorer's hat on! The next step takes you a bit deeper into the mine as you probe into the lives and backgrounds of your central character(s). This is also where you will find answers to some of the questions you raised above.

Warning: set a time limit for yourself. The problem with having so much helpful, colorful material to explore is that, unless you discipline yourself to move on, you will get trapped down in the mine and no one will ever see you again (or benefit from your discoveries). Here is a list of a few of the extrabiblical resources you will want to consult as your time allows. If you can, start buying some of these. Otherwise, your church and public libraries may have copies. A member of your church's pastoral staff would probably let you look in his or her personal library.

1. Concordances. These are great for word studies since a complete concordance lists every verse in the Bible containing a particular word; that way you can study "sanctification," for instance, in different contexts and so gain a deeper understanding of the concept. Try to find a concordance that is based on the version of the Bible you use (e.g., *New American Standard; King James Version; Revised Standard Version of the Bible; Holy Bible, New International Version*).

2. Bible dictionaries. These will give you brief definitions of key people, places, and concepts.

3. Bible encyclopedias. These multivolume reference works will give you more-detailed information on a wider variety of topics than a single-volume Bible dictionary. Bible encyclopedias also often contain helpful bibliographies for more in-depth study.

4. Cross-reference tools. R.A. Torrey's *The Treasury of Scripture Knowledge* is a good resource, offering 500,000 Scripture references and parallel passages that can help you gain a deeper understanding of and appreciation for your story.

5. Commentaries. *The Bible Knowledge Commentary* is concise, true to the text and, through its many charts and diagrams, helpful in providing an overview of each book of the Bible as well as many Bible doctrines.

6. Histories. Here consider New and Old Testament surveys as well as more-restrictive histories, such as ones dealing with the time of the Judges or the Patriarchs, the Divided Kingdom or the Apostolic Age. Alfred Edersheim's *Life and Times of Jesus the Messiah* is an old history but a gem.

7. Articles. Check out your local library or seminary for specialized magazines and journals which contain articles on the subject of your story.

8. Atlas. *The Moody Atlas of Bible Lands* locates major geographical features and provides helpful commentary on

those passages where geography plays a vital role. For example, the exodus from Egypt and the conquest of Canaan take on new life when you see the kind of hostile terrain the Israelites had to negotiate.

There are certainly other guides we could have mentioned, but these will give you some biblical meat to chew on for a while. As you are beginning to see, the problem is not going to be "Will I have enough to say?" Rather, the question for the serious Bible student is "How can I possibly get it all in?" Or to put it negatively, "What do I leave out?"

The answer to that question is really simple: If the new bit of information you've found doesn't contribute significantly to your message, then leave it out. Think back to the Rembrandt painting and ask yourself, "Do my listeners really need to see that much detail in the peripheral material, or is it merely distracting them from the thrust of the message?"

We must be severe, merciless in slicing away the fat from our story. No contraband prose allowed on board! Toss that cargo into a file folder and use it another day! No "sacred cow" pages, paragraphs, lines, or letters! Prune away those flowery passages to make room for more fruitful and efficient writing. No By-path Meadows (regardless how lovely) will lure us away from the straight and narrow path of the story. Stick to the essential points. Illuminate those important parts and let the other details fade into the background. More on editing when we get to the chapter on writing.

Now it is time to begin a character analysis of the main characters themselves in some detail (as much as you have time for). Start with the details gleaned from the text. Then use your concordance to find other stories about or references to your character in other parts of Scripture. After the concordance, you may wish to consult a good Bible encyclopedia, commentary, or even a biographical novel that is based on careful research. Be discriminating, since such novels are rare.

Watch out for "biblical" films, especially those made by secular production companies. Few, if any, are even close to being faithful to the biblical storyline, and they often miss the point of the stories they are trying to portray. The goal of the filmmaker is to make money by entertaining his audience, not to be true to the text. Watch biblical films for entertainment but not for accuracy. Remember, your goal is to reconstruct a personality based on a combination of historical fact and a sanctified imagination.

The "gaps" you fill in with your imagination must be plausible, based on your biblical and background research. There's enough shallow writing going on out there to last into the 22nd century. You must join the small but growing band of those committed to integrity and accuracy in research. You may tell fewer stories, but the stories you tell will last.

Here are a few specific questions which will help you begin to flesh out a main character for your audience. For a more detailed consideration of character, see the Character and Scene Analysis outline on page 123.

1. What is your character's religious background?
2. Was your character raised in a well-to-do home or was he or she economically deprived?
3. What is your character's educational background?
4. What is your character's age?
5. List your main character's physical characteristics.
   a. What is your character's height?
   b. Can you guess how much he or she may have weighed?
   c. Is hair color or length mentioned?
6. Is your character in good physical condition?

Of course, you will not reveal most of this information in the story itself, but the better you know the main character, the more authentic the story will be. Think about how this familiarity works in real life. Persons who have been married to their spouses for many years find themselves thinking the way their spouses think. They anticipate their responses, find themselves completing their sentences, or thinking the same thoughts at the same time. When others want to know something about either spouse, they talk to the other, because who knows better?

Make the effort to know your characters well. A confident, relaxed quality will come to your storytelling as a result. And whatever you share about your characters, however little, will ring true to your audience.

Now I have a lot of facts and a lot of observations. How do I know which ones are important enough to include and which ones I should leave out?

This is a question of interpretation. Time to take off your explorer's hat for the time being and don the judge's wig. Now you are going to judge which details are important and which are not. Ask yourself, "What lesson is this story teaching?" If, for example, you were looking at your observations from 1 Samuel 17, you might conclude that the lesson or point of the story would have something to do with our need to put our trust in God rather than measuring our ability by the size of our opponent. (Notice the emphasis on Israel's fear because of the outward appearance of Goliath; Goliath made the same mistake in looking at David and assuming his victory, based on David's outward appearance.)

As you are doing research on the background of David, you will discover almost immediately that he was chosen by the Lord not according to his outward appearance but because of his heart relationship with Him (1 Sam. 16:1-13). Since the fight with Goliath occurs in the very next chapter, it would seem the author is making a point about not judging by outward appearance.

When you note that Israel is afraid of a giant (17:11), you may recall another time in Israel's history when giants struck a chord of fear in the hearts of God's people. Remember a place called Kadesh Barnea? Israel couldn't forget. The people were on the verge of entering the land of promise. Then they saw the giants, and that was the last the giants saw of them (Num. 13:30-33). The Israelites blew their chance. They paid the price for their lack of trust in God by wandering in the wilderness for 40 years. How many days did Goliath come out to taunt the armies of the living God? Forty days (1 Sam. 17:16). Hm-m-m. Interesting coincidence. Or maybe it's more than coincidence. Maybe God used those 40 days of bullying to remind them — one day for each year of their wandering due to their cowardice before the giants in the land. Do you think the Israelites would have remembered? Do you think they would have felt ashamed? Imagine yourself in their position.

Why did Eliab burst out at David as he did? This wasn't the first time David had been to the camp, for he "went back and forth from Saul to tend his father's sheep at Bethlehem"(17:15); and yet this is the first recorded outburst by one of David's brothers. Put yourself in Eliab's sandals. Would you have been on edge if you had been made fun of for 40 days — and you were scared of dying, to boot? If so, tell us. Better yet, show us. Let us remember with Eliab and the other soldiers; let us feel the shame with them as you tell the story. Look for other details that help sharpen the focus of the story. They help us see clearly and vividly the lesson the story has for all of us.

You won't have trouble figuring out which details to keep in and which to kick out once you have decided on the lesson of the story. Going through the details, praying for God to illumine their significance to you, and seeing the connections between these events and others within the larger story of the Bible — these are all part of the process of interpretation. Then it's simply a matter of developing those details which enhance or contribute in some way to the development of the story's lesson.

Now that I know my main character(s) and the lesson of the story, how should I address the audience? More specifically, should I take them back in time, or should I come to them in the present?

You may decide to tell the story as a narrator who is detached from the story. That is, you don't portray a character in the story but you tell the story from the viewpoint of a historian or biographer. You are essentially an interested observer. If you tell the story from this perspective or "point of contact," you are simply a more-informed member of the audience, and you relate the story from a third-person, thoroughly objective posture. It would be most akin to telling the story from the viewpoint of the author of the story, though you probably won't assume a character other than your own. Though Moses wrote Genesis, for example, you wouldn't pretend to be Moses. You would still be yourself.

 But let's say you want to bring the story to life even more. Let's imagine you decide to relate the story through the eyes of one of the characters in the story. You have three basic options with regard to how you might address any audience. First, you may want the character to speak to your listeners as if they have traveled back in time to his day and are a part of his culture. If you decide on this option, the audience becomes part of the action of the story. An example of this kind of interaction may be seen in Reg Grant's narrative "Something to Steal," in which the audience is addressed as a group of fellow prisoners.

This option of taking your listeners back in time has the advantage of their immediate involvement — they become a part of the story. If you choose this option, you will want to have an introduction and/or a conclusion typed out to give to the host (this may be the pastor or the Sunday School teacher). Don't rely on the host to "work something up" for you. You never know what you'll get! Play it safe and take the pressure off both of you.

In the second option, the character tells the story as if he or she has traveled from biblical times to relate the story to a present-day audience. The storyteller in this case almost always maintains greater objectivity than in the "audience as participant" model above. He or she often relates the story from a divine viewpoint; that is, the character is in possession of all the facts and can relate the story with as little subjective bias as possible.

One advantage of telling the story from this point of contact is that the storyteller takes on the aura of a sage, the wise one who has learned from his or her experience and has had the luxury of time to reflect on the lesson the story has for us all. Another advantage is the variety of levels the storyteller can explore in telling the story. He or she may drift in and out of the scene while reliving the event. The more real it becomes to the storyteller recalling it, the more involved the audience will become in the action of the narrative, and the more susceptible they will be to the lesson that emerges. Take a look at John Reed's "Gideon" for an example of how this works.

The danger, as one might expect, lies in the possibility of cool detachment from the passion of the narrative. The storyteller can become so clinical in his dissection of the story that it becomes a bloodless cadaver. The result: a coroner's autopsy rather than a resurrection of a biblical character.

A third option for a point of contact is to allow the audience to witness a dramatic re-creation of the event, much as an audience would watch a stage play. In this case, the scene is re-created as if it were really happening before the eyes of the audience. The storyteller is totally involved in the action of the scene and appears to be unaware of any audience. One advantage of this form of presentation is that the audience senses a reality to the scene — as if they were getting to peak through a crack in time to see how it really was. The viewers feel that they are able to make their own judgments and come to their own conclusions. "Abraham and Isaac" by John Reed is an example of a story told from this point of contact.

A weakness in this option is that the viewers can become detached more easily than in either of the other two. They are afforded the luxury of being spectators since they are never acknowledged as an audience. They can sit in judgment, without running the risk of becoming involved in the story.

Audiences feel safer and more relaxed in this most conventional of storytelling forms. It's like watching TV or a movie. Interaction, audiences feel, is neither expected nor appropriate. Our objective as storytellers is to draw them in unawares, though, and not allow them to kick back in their padded seats. Our stories must challenge them to judge the characters in the story *and* that part of themselves they see in them.

These three basic options may be interwoven. For example, you may have *asides* (lines spoken either directly to an audience or to oneself) within the third option above (which does not, as a rule, acknowledge the audience as such). Or, you may begin by addressing the audience directly, and then as you tell the story, become so engrossed in the scene that you temporarily "forget" there is an audience, and relive that part of the story before them. Whichever option you decide on, don't let it become a straitjacket; rather, let it become a suit which you tailor to fit your needs and those of your audience.

In this chapter we considered the components of the first "R" of dramatic storytelling: reading. We found that by simply reading the text and making a few observations, we can discover the essential ingredients of any story. We excavated the text with five tools: who, when, where, why, and how. Then we went deeper into the mine, examining the rich background of the story found in extrabiblical literature. Detailed character analysis topped off our look into the fine points of the story. We wrapped it up with a consideration of three basic options for addressing the story to the audience: (1) take the audience back in time; (2) bring the storyteller to the present time; (3) allow the audience to witness the historical event through a "time window." Next, we will discover how to translate all this good groundwork into words that will stick in any heart.

FOUR

The Second "R" of Storytelling: 'Riting

I'm really not a writer. As a matter of fact, the last time I wrote something I was still in school! But I'd love to learn how to write a story I could tell to someone. Where do I start?

Let's assume at this point that you have decided on the story you want to tell, that you have done the necessary background study, and that you have decided on the point of contact you wish to adopt. The first step in writing is the easiest because it doesn't involve putting any words on paper at all!

The first step in writing is to imagine. Here is a fundamental principle that will apply not only to the writing process but to the telling process as well: See it before you write it. (When we get into telling the story, the principle will become: See it before you say it.) Imagine what the scenes in the story must have looked like. See the story of David and Goliath unfold through David's eyes.

Don't limit yourself to sight imagery. Explore the other senses as well: the aroma of the bread Jesse baked for David's older brothers, the heaviness of Saul's armor, the texture of the five smooth stones, the sound of Goliath's voice echoing in the valley, the taste of David's sweat as he ran from Jerusalem to the Valley of Elah. The more you draw on the senses, the more listeners will be drawn into the story and the greater its effect will be on them. Imagine the scene in as much detail as you can. See the leaves on the trees. What kinds of trees are they? Feel the water of the brook. Is it cold? What color are the stones you gather? After you have explored the scene in detail, you are ready for the second step:

Write.

Take the pencil, pen, or keyboard and begin writing words. At this point, you put on the explorer's hat again. Do not judge the quality of your writing—just write! Good things happen when you begin to write which cannot happen until you begin. You will be amazed at what goes onto the paper or computer screen in front of you.

If you get stuck or feel as though your creative battery is dead, there's an easy way to give yourself a jump start. Simply pretend to be one of your major characters.

Let's say you are going to tell the story through David's eyes; ask yourself a specific question about one of your experiences (remember now, you are David). How did you feel about tending your father's sheep while your older brothers were off fighting the enemy? Describe the sheep. Remember the smell. Think about the life of a shepherd—hot during the day and cold at night. Describe your battle with one of the lions that attacked the fold. Talk about your relationship with Eliab as you were growing up. Write about anything that would help your audience see David's world through David's eyes. Don't worry about following the storyline yet. That will come as you write more.

What is the control on the writing at this point? What keeps it from becoming random? Your theme. This is not chaotic writing—your thoughts are swirling like electrons around a nucleus idea (to borrow a concept from Gabrielle Ricos' excellent book, *Writing the Natural Way*, J.P. Tarcher, Inc.). Your thoughts on paper may begin in what appears to be a random fashion, but don't trust appearances—keep writing!

Before long (probably within the first 10–15 minutes of actual writing), you will begin to sense a structure emerging. At this point, you may want to sketch a brief story outline. It won't be set in concrete (you can always modify it later), but at least the outline paints in broad brushstrokes the form of the story. Any story will have at least three parts: a beginning, a middle, and an end. Or to think of it a bit more organically, every story has roots (the beginning), a trunk (the middle), and some leafy branches (the end). Try translating these main parts and any others into the turning points of the story.

In the beginning of your story, you will want to sink your roots down into the soil of the setting. Make sure listeners know where you are (and where they are if they are a part of the story). If you are telling the story through David's eyes, your first point may look something like this:

I.   David takes bread to his brothers fighting the Philistines in the Valley of Elah.

The roots of your story will help listeners understand the situation as David understood it. They will share in his excitement as he runs expectantly to the battle lines to see his big brothers in the great army of Saul defeat the pagan Philistines. Here you may wish to hint at your theme: Don't judge by outward appearances.

As he crosses the hills on the way to his brothers, David may be thinking about the size and reputation of the Philistine army; or perhaps he had just killed a lion or bear and he can't wait to tell his brothers. Whatever you choose, it should prepare the audience for the lesson ahead.

Now you are ready for the middle part, the trunk of the tree. This is usually the longest of the three parts, just as the trunk is the longest part of the tree. Remember, look for shifts in the action of the story in order to find the main points in the outline. The next major point in the story focuses on David's fight with Goliath. So your second main point might read:

II.   David defeats Goliath.

How do I know where to begin a section like this?

Look for turning points in the action. For example, the turning point between points I and II in the David and Goliath story would occur when David decides to volunteer to fight Goliath in 17:32. You might want to include this observation as (A) under point II. Point II, then, would state in broad terms what happens in this part of the story. How it begins to unfold would be revealed in (A).

II.   David defeats Goliath.
    A.   Saul sends for David.
    B.   David volunteers to fight Goliath.

Under point II you would describe the giant through David's

eyes. All the detail that we had to skip over in 1 Samuel 17:4-7 can come to light now as David faces the giant for the first time. How does he see the giant differently than the Israelite army saw him? Remember, they were on the surrounding hills looking down on Goliath. David saw all nine feet of him at ground level!

You will find that the middle part of your story will have more detail and more concentrated action, but that the focus of that detail and action is pretty narrow. It's as if you were zooming in with a camcorder for a close-up of the fight. The closer you get, the more detail you see, as your focus is concentrated on the life-and-death struggle between a boy and a giant. You enter their thoughts and reveal strategies and feelings, all of which you select in order to highlight the theme of the story.

Finally, David vanquishes Goliath (turning point) and you are ready to put the top on your tree. This last and briefest part of your story will reveal the effect of David's victory.

III.   David's victory over Goliath leads to an Israelite rout of the terrified Philistine army.

Be careful not to overdevelop this third section. It is probably the best place of all to bring home the lesson that David learned from his encounter with the giant. You may wish to have him close out the story by reflecting back on how Samuel selected him over his brothers. There he discovered that "the Lord does not look at the things man looks at. Man looks at the outward appearance, but the Lord looks at the heart" (1 Sam. 16:7).

Later, as you memorize the story, you will translate the above outline points and subpoints into acts and scenes. More about that in chapter 5. As a general rule, your audience will remember the last line of the last section better and longer than any other line in your story. So make it count! You don't always have to save the "lesson line" for the very end, but bear in mind that you can't afford to waste the last thing your listeners will hear you say since that is what they are likely to remember best.

When you begin filling in the outline (that is, when you begin to write the script), you may feel drawn to write the end or the climax of the story first. That's great! In fact, we recommend it. Writing the end of the story first is like drawing the bull's-eye before you shoot the arrow — it gives you a target. It keeps you from shooting arrows off in all directions. If you know how the story ends, you know where the parts are going.

Now make everything else you write move the story along toward that ending. Remember, the key at this point is to get words on paper; you will polish later. If you have the rough draft of the story down on paper, you are ready for the next step: Rewriting.

As every good writing teacher will tell you, the essence of writing is rewriting. Why? Think of it this way: a deflated beachball is nothing. Its essence — what makes it a beachball — is missing. A beachball will not realize its potential while it remains flat. In the same way, your writing will not fulfill its potential until you breath life into it by rewriting.

Rewriting is one of the most painful points in the process, but it is crucial. It's painful because you have to shed all the fat prose, toss all those pretty verbal flourishes overboard like so much contraband. You have to whip those lazy verbs and overweight nouns into shape!

In this step, you again exchange your explorer's hat for the judge's wig. You are now about the business of assaying your original collection of treasured sentences and paragraphs. Be prepared for some shocks. What you had believed to be pure storytelling gold may, under closer analysis, turn out to be only fool's gold — words that look good on the page and sound good to the ear, but are of no real value. Chances are you may already have a bit of fool's gold littering your prose.

Simpering Verbs

These are the whiners — the tuneless, toady words that haven't the energy to hop, much less hightail it. Why settle for words that make your story chug along on regular when high-octane verbs are available for a few pennies worth of extra effort? It's an exercise that never gets old, never withers.

Why say Saul "hid" when you can say he "cowered"? Did Goliath "call out" in the midst of the Valley of Elah or did he "bellow"? Do clouds simply "move" across the sky; or do they "sail," "scud," or "slip"? The fog doesn't "come"; it "creeps," it "devours," it "blankets."

You say your vocabulary is a tad lifeless — like a dead worm? No problem! Buy and use a good thesaurus. J.I. Rodale publishes a good one called *The Synonym Finder*.

But let's say you have a bit of a different challenge. You are trying to describe how the wind moved through an ancient Roman prison. You need just the right verb to go with the noun "wind." Where are you going to look? Try *The Word Finder* (again, published by J.I. Rodale). Look up the word "wind," and you will discover no fewer than 71 verbs that go with it. And in case you are stumped for a modifier for wind, *The Word Finder* suggests 222 adjectives you can use to capture the kind of movement you have in mind. Carl Sandburg valued living prose and said, "I should like to think that as I go on writing there will be sentences truly alive, with verbs quivering, with nouns giving color and echoes."

Hairless Nouns

These formless abstractions lie there on the page like gray slugs. There's only one thing to do when you find a slug on your page — scrape it off!

Suppose you are telling the story of the stoning of Stephen. Was it a "crowd of people" who gathered to murder him, or was it a "mob"? Was Solomon a "husband" to the maiden in the Song of Solomon, or was he her "lover"? Did Satan take Christ to the "top" of the temple, or to its "pinnacle"? Did Moses hear the "sound" of God on Mount Sinai, or did he hear His "thunder"? Be specific. Be concrete. Be precise and uncompromising in your choice of nouns. As Mark Twain said, "Choose the right word and not its second cousin."

Snooty Modifiers

The role of modifier is an exalted one deserving careful attention. Storytellers need to be particularly wary of gaudy pretenders to this noble office. Often they stand in the wings, whimpering like the spoiled child star who wants always to be in the spotlight, regardless of whose scene it is. Many of the more familiar adjectives have been so mauled by pretentious admen that people have come to distrust these words. These are the "un" words — the words that "un-impress." (Everything from cars to laundry detergents claims to be the "best," "enriched," or [my un-favorite] "new and improved".)

Good adjectives dress your nouns and pronouns elegantly, enhancing their natural beauty without drawing attention to themselves. Adjectives should function like good Christians; they are there not to be served, but to serve.

Sooty Modifiers

Sooty adjectives are too tired to even pretend to be genuine. They have become frayed and shabby from overwork. Any original luster has long since faded. For years, adjectives like "swell," "good," "fine," "nice," and "bad" (which can now mean "good," by the way) have been dragged through the verbal muck of small minds. Their brilliance dulled, they have become pedestrian. If such an adjective retains any luminescence now, it is only mortgaged from a brighter noun; it is merely a pale moon reflecting the borrowed light from a distant sun.

Be wary of these old beggars. They will squeeze all the freshness out of your story, leaving it shriveled and gasping for breath. In particular, watch out for the marriage of anemic verbs ("is," "are") to listless adjectives. Their union will only produce sentences that whimper and limp along the page, infecting all the decent nouns that lie in their path. Avoid these tired adjectives.

Not all inappropriate adjectives are haughty or hackneyed. Some truly delightful adjectives have been deflowered (like the word "gay"). Others have simply been ignored: Brobdingnagian (huge) has become Lilliputian (diminutive) in its usage (no "swift" change, this). In general, we would do well to heed the implicit advice of Sandburg when he noted, "At 61 I am more suspicious of adjectives than at any other time in all my born days!"

Writing for the Ear

Remember, you are writing a story for the ear, not for the eye. These words will be heard; they will be felt. Well-chosen words are flaming arrows that can pierce the breastplate of indifference to thaw a cryogenic heart. You will begin to notice as you rewrite that certain words seem to fit better together simply because they sound better together. Sentences have rhythms just as music has rhythms. There is a beat or cadence to well-crafted sentences that makes them easy to hear and easier to remember. Find the tempo. Discover the music and let it rinse through your words clear as rain.

Now you have the story down on paper. Congratulations! Major progress! It's time to take a chance with it. Time for the fourth point in the writing process:

Test out your story on a friend.

You feel a combination of nervous excitement and consuming fear. You hope your friend will like it, but you still wonder. This is your baby! You've nursed it, pampered it, molded and shaped it. Now you're about to let a friend sit in judgment on it. And this isn't just any friend. This is the most brutally honest friend you have — the one who will tell it like it is, the one you always thought was a bit blunt when it came to offering an opinion. Only storytellers ask for this kind of abuse!

So, here you go. You read your story in your best voice, taking time to let all the word pictures soak in. You notice out of the corner of your eye that your one-person audience isn't moving much. That could mean only one of two things: your friend has either fallen in love with it or has fallen asleep. Keep going!

David has his sling in hand; he lets the stone fly — Goliath's down! The Philistine forces gasp, then scream, then run! Great victory! Great lesson! But was it a great story?

You wait for a response. Your friend leans forward, looks you right in the eye, and says, "You know, the part I liked best was . . ." You find out what went well and where the weak spots are. Sure enough, despite your best efforts, you spent a bit too long on developing the last point. Your friend felt that you were preaching a bit. And some of that stuff about David's relationship with his brothers in the beginning was interesting, but it didn't seem all that important to the story you wanted to tell. Save it — maybe it would work better in another story. Now you are ready for the final point in good story-writing: Editing.

Sometimes I feel guilty about "editing" the biblical story to make it fit the needs of my audience. Is it OK to leave out some details of the story?

Yes. In fact, you can't tell the story exactly the way it happened because even the men who wrote the Bible didn't include *all* the details. They chose to highlight certain events for our instruction. When you tell a Bible story you begin with a true, though abbreviated, account of an event. In the telling, you expose the lesson of the story for listeners by subtly punctuating those points which will enable them to see not only the historical event but its significance for them today.

How can I make sure the students will understand the lesson the story is trying to get across?

By definition, stories do not preach. In storytelling, we are working at the level of illustrations and their implications. Lest you think that is bad, take a look at how seldom Jesus was strictly didactic ("teachy") and how often He wrapped His truth in a savory story.

In his excellent book *The Parables of Jesus*, Dr. Dwight Pentecost notes, "Approximately one-third of Christ's teaching as recorded in the Gospels was in the form of parables."[1] Notice how brief the parables are, but how stuffed with common sense. Jesus didn't need a lot of words to get His message across. His stories were simple meals for the heart and mind. He broke down massive truth into bite-sized morsels so His hearers could digest it a little bit at a time. And He always left them hungry for more. You, therefore, should keep the story short and the lesson simple and memorable.

You will rarely find a script that can't be improved by cutting. This is the final polish, the last buffing away of any rough spots. So take your friend's advice to heart as you take a last critical look at the story. Is there anything superfluous? Have you strayed from the path into some lovely (and equally distracting) "meadow"? Do your verbs resonate? What about the nouns? Can you see what you are talking about? Can you smell it, taste it, hear it, feel it? Do your modifiers enrich or do they upstage? Is your theme focused and clear without being preachy? Are your sentences short and memorable where they need to be? If the words don't work, cut them out. Sacrifice those "sacred cow" lines, words, and syllables on the altar of efficiency (use a red pen to edit—it gets the blood pumping).

After all is said and done, how long should my story be?

Think of a story like a well-tailored suit. If properly fashioned, it will fit one audience (or at least one type of audience) better than any other, and will be most appropriate and effective in a particular setting. This rule applies to the content of the story, of course, but it also applies to the duration of the performance. Here are a couple of variables to keep in mind when trying to decide on the length of your tale.

Age of the audience. A basic rule of thumb: the younger, the shorter. Tailor the length of the story to the size of the listeners. Trying to force a well-made grown-up story on a bunch of second-graders is a lot like putting Saul's armor on David—it just doesn't fit the need.

Occasion. If you are telling a story for a Sunday School class (figuring on 35–40 minutes of actual teaching time in an average Sunday School class) and you want to save some time for questions and observations, your story will need to be pretty short (meaning anywhere from 1–5 minutes). Consider the stories of our Lord. As we noted above, more than 30 percent of all His New Testament teaching was in the form of parables—short parables. Even the longest of them (the Parable of the Prodigal Son from Luke 15) would not have taken Jesus more than three and a half minutes to tell from beginning to end. Stories need not be long to be effective. In an adult Sunday School class your story can be as short as you wish, but should probably not go over 25 minutes maximum. Optimum length seems to work out to 15–20 minutes.

Why so short? Attention span (theirs) and life span (yours). Your audience lacks the listening time and you lack the preparation time. Remember, you are telling stories to a group that has an appetite for high-tech special effects and is used to skipping across galaxies at the speed of light. The union of technological sophistication and cultural illiteracy has bred a generation with a shrinking attention span.

Keep in mind too that, more often than not, story length is inversely proportional to preparation time. The shorter story often demands more work than a longer story relating the same event. In a shorter story you exercise greater discretion in selecting the story elements and greater control in writing and telling. So don't bite off more than you can chew or they can digest.

Should I always write out a separate introduction and conclusion?

It's always a good idea to have an introduction and a few concluding remarks typed up for your host. You will almost certainly regret it if you depend on him or her to remember that Esther was a Jewish princess in a pagan court during the fifth century B.C.! They will be doing well if they remember your name, so take the pressure off them and supply a sheet to read that will set up the story properly.

The same rule applies to conclusions. You may tell a story where it would be inappropriate for the character to offer an invitation, but it would be perfectly fine for the host to follow up your story with an invitation to accept Christ.[2] Provide the exact words for your host to say—not just an outline or suggestions. Supply the exact words. This is the voice of painful experience speaking. You never know what will come out when you leave your host to the mercy of his own unpreparedness!

---

[1]J. Dwight Pentecost, *The Parables of Jesus* (Grand Rapids, Mich.: Zondervan Publishing House, 1982), p. 14.
[2]See Reg Grant's "Something to Steal" in the appendix for an example of a story that works well with a separate introduction and conclusion.

FIVE

The Third "R" of Storytelling: Rehearsing

Your story is written and polished. You have tried it out on a friend and he or she loved it. You have seen the event through the eyes of a main character; you have entered into the story. Now it's time to get the story inside you. The goal of rehearsal is mastery of *all* the elements of the story. So, at the very least, mastery means you know the story itself cold. Mastery of all the elements begins with mastery of structure, the most basic element of the story.

But you, the storyteller (your body, your emotions, your voice), are a key element in storytelling as well. After all, what's a story without a storyteller? Therefore, mastery also means you know when, where, and why you are going to move as you tell the story. You know when your voice should be soft and when it should be hard. Mastery means you know what to do with your hands, eyes, and feet. In short, mastering the story means more than memorizing the words; it means controlling the body, the voice, and the emotions of the storyteller as well.

Once the story is mastered—once all the mechanical obligations of research, writing, and rehearsal have been fulfilled—you will be free to enter into the story again each time you tell it. Fail to master the story, and you will be shackled to the manuscript, uncertain of what to say, how to say it, or what to do with your hands. Uncertainty breeds fear. If you are hesitant, uncertain, fearful of forgetting the next part of the story, your audience will be uneasy as well. Mastery, however, generates confidence both in you and in your audience. The goal of rehearsal is mastery of the story and the storyteller. Let's rehearse.

I have trouble remembering my phone number. Do I have to memorize the whole story word for word?

It depends on the form of the story you are telling. If you are telling a story in the form of a poem (there are thousands of wonderful story poems out there, waiting for you to discover them), then word-for-word memorization is essential. Let's say you are reciting Robert W. Service's "The Cremation of Sam Magee." You would not want to substitute your own words for those of Service since the cadence and imagery of the poem are so dependent on his words.

On the other hand, if you are telling a story you have written in prose, you may find that word-for-word memorization is too much of a hassle. If this is the case, you will want to have the story's lesson and major turning points firmly fixed in your mind so that you will be able to tell the story with great naturalness and honesty. There can be a great deal more to memorization, but there must never be less. Just remember, the greater control you have of the details of the story, the greater confidence you will have when it comes time to tell it. If you can recall the story word for word, you will be able to recall the major turning points. For that reason, we will show you how to recall the entire story letter perfect!

What is the best way to memorize the story?

Step one: Break the story down into acts and scenes. Each act and each scene will have a beginning, a middle, and an end. Often the acts will correspond to the major outline points in the story. Each act is composed of short scenes. To begin, let's work in the scenes. In the first act of the David and Goliath story, for example, there are several scenes. While you may decide to fill in the gaps when you write your story, let's look at how these scenes would break down if we just followed the story strictly from the text.

Act I. David takes bread to his brothers fighting the Philistines in the Valley of Elah.
     A. (Scene 1) David receives food and instructions from his father Jesse (1 Sam. 17:17-19).
     B. (Scene 2) David travels to the camp (17:20a).

C. (Scene 3) David arrives at the camp and greets his brothers (17:20b-22).
D. (Scene 4) David sees Goliath for the first time and witnesses Israel's response (17:23-25).
E. (Scene 5) David finds out what will be done for the man who kills Goliath (17:25-27).
F. (Scene 6) David's brother Eliab accuses him of coming only to watch the fighting (17:28).

Each scene may be only a few lines long—not difficult to memorize at all. But you're not quite ready to begin memory work yet.

Step two: Go back through the scenes you have just marked off and see if there is a dominant emotion portrayed in each scene. We might label the first major scene as "exuberance" because, from the beginning of the scene to its climax, David emerges as high-spirited and exuberant in marked contrast to the cowering Israelite army.

The other scenes may have dominant emotions, though these will often overlap or continue from scene to scene. Scenes 1, 2, and 3 would exhibit a growing anticipation on David's part of getting into the thick of the action. Scene 4 reveals wonder at the size and message of Goliath. Scene 5 unveils the righteous anger of David toward Goliath, and Scene 6 flashes with unrighteous anger in the exchange between David and Eliab. Now you are ready to plan your movement.

Wait a minute. I thought I was supposed to be memorizing by now.

Think of it this way. Memorizing a story is like planting a crop. If you throw your seed out onto hard earth, you aren't going to get much of a return on your investment. But if you prepare the ground ahead of time so that it's ready to receive the seed, your harvest will be rich and full. What you are doing now by planning your movement in the scene is preparing the soil. Following these steps will save you hours of frustration in the memorizing process. Hang in there! Only one more step to go.

Step three: Block out the scene. Blocking means indicating on a piece of paper where you are going to move while you are telling the story.

Why should I want to move while I tell the story? Wouldn't that be distracting?

It would be distracting if your movements were random and without purpose. Here's another rule of thumb: Every movement you make will either add to or detract from the overall effectiveness of your story. So you want to take advantage of the best, most appropriate movement in order to achieve maximum effectiveness. Block out your storytelling area on a diagram into six equal parts:

Audience
Front of Stage or Platform

AREA 4	AREA 1	AREA 3
AREA 6	AREA 2	AREA 5

Blocking Diagram

The psychology of aesthetics tells us that audiences respond instinctively and uniquely to each area of the stage as marked off above. They perceive each block as relatively "strong" or "weak," "cool" or "warm." You can assign the scenes of your story to each area accordingly.

The six areas are numbered in order of "strength." As a general rule, the closer you are to your audience, the stronger the impression you will make. The farther away you are, the more remote you will seem. As you face the audience, scenes played to your right (stage right) will tend to be warmer emotionally, while scenes played to your left (stage left) will tend to be cooler.

Now that you have identified the dominant emotional tone of

Audience

AREA 4	AREA 1	AREA 3
Cool Distress, Conflict (Ex., David's argument with Eliab)	Medium Confrontational (Ex., David's fight with Goliath)	Warm Intimate (Ex., David praying to the Lord as he picks up the stones.)
AREA 6	AREA 2	AREA 5
Cold Extreme Alienation (Ex., Death of Goliath)	Medium Distant, Aloof (Ex., David arriving at the camp)	Warm More "Distant" (Ex., David's smaller scene with Jesse)

each of the scenes, try placing the scenes in the appropriate boxes on your blocking diagram. You may wish to have one blocking diagram per major scene or outline point.

You are going through the process of mastering the material even as you decide where to place your short scenes. One word of caution: don't move into a new or different block simply because the emotion of the scene changes. The blocked-out areas do not dictate that you *must* move; they merely suggest that, if movement is appropriate, they would probably be the best places to play out the scene.

You must have a logical reason for a move into a new area. As the storyteller, you may sense a need to move that your character does not share. Let's say that David is in Area 5 receiving instructions from his father Jesse. You, the storyteller, know that he needs to move into Area 2 for the next scene. So you locate the army of Israel in Area 2. Where else would David go?

You help your characters by arranging and structuring the different elements of your story in such a way that movement from one area to another is natural rather than forced. The worst reason to move is because you have to change areas, while the best movement is the inevitable one.

Here is an easy way to block your text on a sheet of paper so you can rehearse with it in hand. Keep the typed copy of your story in a three-ring binder. Be sure to double- or even triple-space when you type it out. Then draw blocking charts on blank sheets of paper and place them in the notebook opposite each typed page of the story. Write "Audience" above the charts and label the blocks Areas 1–6 accordingly. In this way, when you carry the notebook onto the stage for rehearsals, the text and the corresponding movements will be right before you.

Now draw an X on the chart at the point where you wish to begin speaking. If you were performing the story of David and Goliath, your first X would be in Area 5, the block in the lower right-hand corner.

Audience

David and Goliath
Act 1, scenes 1–6

After David has received instructions from Jesse, he will move into Area 2 and probably a bit closer to the audience (see chart above). You can indicate this move by a line beginning at X and ending where you wish to stop in Area 2. Suppose you wish to move when you reach the word "went." In your manuscript, then, put a *1* (for the first move) over the word "went." On your blocking page, place a *1* at the spot where you intend to play out the next scene. In the third scene, David may move into Area 3 to greet his brothers. The fourth scene would find

70

him in Area 1, seeing Goliath right out over the heads of the people in the back row. David moves over to the edge of Area 4 to play out the fifth scene, then into the center of Area 4 for the confrontation with Eliab in the sixth scene. There he will play out the last scene in the first act.

Draw on a blocking chart *only* the moves that you will make while telling the opposite page of the story. On successive blocking charts, mark an X to show your position on stage as you start the next page of the story. If you make no moves on a given page of the story, the opposite blocking chart will have only an X showing where you are. Remember to write the numbers of the moves over the words (or at the places) in the manuscript where you wish to move.

Once you have decided where you should be and why you should be there, you have blocked your story. Now you are ready to memorize.

The best way to remember your story is to associate your lines with areas and physical movements. Whenever possible, get on your feet and walk the story through according to your blocking. When you can't walk it through physically, do so mentally. Imagine the audience in front of you. Carry your notebook, especially in the beginning, and follow your blocking. If it doesn't feel natural, adjust accordingly. Try moving on a different word or a different sentence. Nothing is set in concrete. Stay flexible.

How much should I memorize at one time?

Take one small scene at a time. Read all the words off the page for that scene. Read the scene through out loud 20 to 30 times. Then say the first line without looking at the text. Once you have it cold, move on to the second line, and say it with the first line. Progress through the scene until you have the whole scene under your belt. There may be some minor movement within the scene, but you will want to save the major movements for scene breaks in order to help punctuate the story's action. Before you know it, you will have the first act down.

Pace yourself. Don't try to memorize a whole act in one evening if you don't feel like it. Each person is different, so don't push yourself too hard. Take it slowly and enjoy it. Memorizing is hard work, but this initial investment of your time will yield great dividends every time you tell the story.

Try reading your story off the manuscript onto a cassette tape. Then play the tape on your way to work, saying the words along with your own voice. You will be amazed at how fast you learn a story this way. Memorize at different times of the day, but especially right before bedtime. For some reason, the mind is stickier right before you go to sleep; you wake up the next morning with the words of your story glued to the frontal lobe. This works great for Bible memory as well.

How much of a stage do I need?

You will seldom have the luxury of a real stage from which you can tell your story, but you can adapt these principles to the size of your storytelling area. We (John and Reg) have told stories in areas as small as four feet square on one occasion (in a living room before the ladies auxiliary), only to tell the same stories the next week on a 60-by-16-foot stage in a hotel ballroom in front of 2,000 people. The principles are the same — simply adapt. If you are working in a confined space, you won't be able to take advantage of staging areas, but you can still achieve variety by addressing different segments of the audience throughout the story.

If I have a medium to large storytelling area, how much of it should I use?

Audiences are like children. They like to have their space defined. As a rule, they aren't comfortable with unstructured space. If you are in a large storytelling area, you may wish to bring something along to help box in the area where your story will be told. A chair, a stump, a bucket — anything that would be natural to the scene and around which the scene may revolve will help define the space for the audience. Once the space has been defined, try to work all of it as you move through the story. Visual variety can enhance the impact of the story if you have done a good job of blocking.

What about gesturing? Are there any rules about what to do with my hands?

After your eyes, the second most expressive parts of your body are your hands. You can use them to help paint a picture for your audience. Think of your fingers as five paint brushes, or as an artist's tools that sculpt images out of thin air. Fingers can pull flowers and triggers. Hands full of fingers can condemn ("Thou art the man!") or inform ("The Philistines? They went that-a-way!"). Hands can invite (Wisdom says, "Let all who are simple come in here!"). Hands can help us picture everything from a tiny mustard seed to an enormous oak. Hands can grasp or caress or pound or clap or chop or pray. You have knuckles to crack and fingers to snap. You can point them like arrows or coil them into fists.

Thumbs too are marvelously versatile creatures. They can hitch a ride, they may preserve (thumbs up) or deny (thumbs down) life to a Roman gladiator. Thumbs may be sucked, smashed, or jammed. And they can cock everything from a musket to a Mauser. Let your story suggest the movement that will help us see the picture that you are seeing. In your hands you have all the equipment needed to help us see any scene vividly.

The question is not "Should I move?" but "When should I move?" There are three and only three times you can move (these rules apply to the smallest gesture and to large movement across the stage (i.e., the blocking we did above): You can move *before* the line, *on* the line, or *after* the line.

How do I know which would be the most effective?

Here's the general rule: What comes first sets up what comes next. In other words, what comes after will automatically have the greater impact and leave the more indelible impression. Let's say you have the line, "Wait, don't go in there!" Your movement is both hands held up to stop the other person. Try it all three ways.

Movement before the line: Hold up hands first, then say, "Wait, don't go in there!" In this case, the line makes the stronger impression since it came last.

Movement on the line: Now the line and the movement are of equal value.

Movement after the line: Now the movement will make the greater impression since it came last.

The decision is still yours to make as to which combination works best. Try them all and go with the one that feels most natural. A carefully thought-through story is almost choreographed. The trick is to make the movements you have planned look unplanned. They must look natural and spontaneous.

How do I achieve that kind of spontaneity?

Rehearsal. The more you rehearse, the less mechanical you will be, both in the delivery of your lines and in your planned movement. Before long, you find yourself moving without having to remind yourself to move.

Moving is sort of like driving a car. You don't have to remind yourself of the required sequence of opening the door, entering, closing the door, fastening the seatbelt, inserting the key, turning it, and shifting into gear. You have formed a habit that is so natural that your body virtually goes on automatic pilot and you find yourself enjoying driving. But don't forget that when you began to learn how to drive you were a bit tense and uneasy. You felt there were so many unnatural rules to remember that you would never get it right. Still, you kept at it until you mastered the mechanics. You can do the same thing in storytelling. There are some rules to get down, but before long you will be cruising!

May I sit down to tell the story? I feel so much more relaxed if I can just sit down.

Usually, carefully planned movement is more visually interesting than a static image (you sitting on a stool). Of course, even sitting on a stool you can use a great deal of your upper torso effectively to communicate images and moods. You may also wish to deliver part of your story (perhaps the beginning and the end) while seated. Remember, visual variety can enhance the effectiveness of the story. Changing height levels is a good way of achieving that variety.

The higher you are, the more prominence you assume. The more-elevated person is the one everyone else is forced to look up to. Conversely, the lowest position assumes the meekest, most subservient posture. Just think of all the different levels you can adopt in your story. You can lie down, sit, squat, crouch, stand, jump, stand on a chair—whatever is appropriate to that part of the story. Experiment! Your audience will delight in the visual variety you offer them as you use different height levels.

My time is so limited. How much rehearsal is necessary?

What you put into your rehearsal is what you will get out of it. Overrehearsing is a possibility, but underrehearsing is much more of a danger for most of us. An ideal plan would allow for a full rehearsal (including blocking, not just running lines) once a day, five days a week for at least three weeks before you tell the story to an audience. You will find yourself going over lines in the shower, on the way to work, and mowing the lawn. That's great, but you need to have that full rehearsal time to discover all the story has to offer.

Adapt the ideal plan for your schedule. Only you know where rehearsal time fits on your list of priorities. Just remember, you usually have a deadline to meet. Decide up front whether you will have adequate time to prepare, then commit accordingly.

How long should each rehearsal be?

Figure on a minimum of 3–5 minutes for every minute of actual story time. If you have a 5-minute story, average rehearsal time will probably be in the neighborhood of 15–25 minutes. For a 10-minute story, you would be rehearsing from 30–50 minutes. If you have more time, grab it.

Should I always rehearse in the same place?

It would be nice if all the full rehearsals could take place in the same location. Ideally, that place would be the actual storytelling area, but reality intrudes and we usually have to settle for our living room when the kids are down for a nap. Do try to rehearse at least once in the actual storytelling area, just so you can get used to the space and so there won't be any visual surprises when you stand up to speak. If it takes going to the church a couple of hours early just to rehearse a couple of times in your area, do it. You'll be glad you did.

Should I rehearse alone, or should I have someone watch me?

In the beginning of the rehearsal period, go it alone. You will have enough on your mind without having to worry about what someone else thinks. Right before you actually tell the story (during the last three or four rehearsals), try the story out on a friend. He or she may see a movement or a gesture that isn't clear. An objective eye is always helpful.

Treat your friend like a regular audience. Don't set the story up by explaining or apologizing. Do it just the way you plan to do it for an audience. That way you will get the most honest response possible.

After your friend tells you how enjoyable the story was, ask if it communicated a lesson. If he or she is able to articulate the lesson of the story, then you've accomplished one of your main goals. If not, then you may have been too obscure or subtle. You will be very vulnerable at this point. If your friend doesn't get your lesson, take it all in stride. Try it out on someone else. But if you get the same response, some more polishing may be in order. Consider reshaping some of the elements to underscore the lesson.

Keep in mind that you aren't simply looking for a pat on the back; you are looking for a discerning eye. Discerning eyes detect flaws as well as appreciate beauty. Hang your ego in the hall closet and get on with the process. God is making you into a storyteller!

Is it better to use props or not?

"Props" is short for "properties" and refers to those items the storyteller uses to enhance his characterization. Props, though, do not include costume, which is a category unto itself. Keep props to a minimum, but don't be afraid to use them. The more props you have, the more elements you have to control. Still, a carefully chosen prop can help bring the character to life.

For example, if you are telling the story of Jacob, and your viewpoint is that of the patriarch himself, you may wish to use a long staff as an aid to the imagination of your audience. The basic rule is: Don't use a prop simply to use a prop; use it to enhance the story and its message. Once you have chosen your prop, use it in every rehearsal. It must be as second nature to you as to the character.

You mentioned costume. Should I wear one or not?

The costume is an option just as props are an option. If the costume is carefully chosen, it can add a great deal to your characterization. We have both told stories of Bible characters in period costumes and in modern clothing. Unless the costume is chosen with great care, it can actually distract from the effectiveness of the story by drawing attention to itself. It may either be too ornate or too makeshift. Coming out in a bathrobe just doesn't cut it for today's sophisticated audiences unless you are doing a comedy or a parody.

In addition, if you are going to get into costume, you really should get into makeup as well. Extended treatment of either subject is beyond the scope of this book. See the bibliography for some suggested books on costuming and makeup. While you're at it, if you really get serious about big-time storytelling, check out a book on theatrical lighting. Good lighting can do wonders to set mood and help establish character and setting— and it needn't be that expensive, especially for a church.

One last word on costuming. In the event that you decide to use a costume, you will probably want to construct your own. It will be cheaper than renting in the long run if you do the story often. Be sure to research the period for authenticity in costuming just as carefully as you researched the background for your interpretation of the event. By all means, begin to work with your costume in your rehearsals as soon as possible. Don't risk saving it for the performance. In fact, don't introduce anything new into the performance. The chances of something going awry are incredibly high.

What about my voice? How do I speak in order to make a story interesting?

"The devil hath not in all his quiver's choice, an arrow for the heart like a sweet voice" (from Lord Byron's *Don Juan,* Canto XV, stanza 13). Good voice begins with good breathing. Make sure you're breathing from your diaphragm and not from your chest. Stand straight and place your right hand on your abdomen, just above your tummy and below your rib cage, and breath in. Your hand should move out as you inhale. Exhale, and your hand moves in. Your chest should move very little if you are breathing correctly.

If you have trouble breathing correctly, try lying on the floor and placing a book on your abdomen. Relax and breathe normally. The book should rise as you inhale and fall as you exhale. With a little practice, you will begin to notice that you have more air to work with. You don't run out of breath at the ends of sentences simply because you are using more of your lung capacity by breathing correctly.

Now that you are breathing correctly, here are a few guidelines for improving voice quality.

Clarity — speak clearly enough to be understood. Make sure you aren't swallowing your words. Imagine that the sound of your words actually starts about two inches in front of your face. This exercise will pull the voice out from the back of the throat to the front of the mouth where it can be clearly understood.

Volume — speak loudly enough to be heard, softly enough to invite attention. Our culture has conditioned audiences to expect amplified voices. Often you will be provided with a microphone for large gatherings, but train as if you will have to rely on your voice alone.

If you do use a microphone, be sure you arrive early enough to check the sound levels with the audio engineer before you tell the story. Doing a sound check with everyone listening is about as inviting as watching the cow butchered for the steak you've ordered. It's a necessary part of the process, but the audience doesn't care to see (or hear) it.

If you will be speaking without amplification, try this old trick on for size. Arrive at the auditorium before anyone else in order to test the acoustics. Speak loudly enough to hear a ring, just a slight echo of your own voice. If your voice rings in an empty auditorium, then your volume will be just about right for a full house.

Articulation — speak distinctly, paying particular attention to your consonants, but avoid being plastic.

Pitch — this has to do with how high or low you speak. Pitch has nothing to do with volume but everything to do with tone. One string on a violin has a higher pitch than another string because it is strung tighter. Similarly, the more tension you have on your vocal folds, the higher the pitch of your voice will be.

To find your optimum pitch, vocalize a yawn and go as deeply as you can without forcing your voice. This low pitch is the most comfortable sound your voice can make. It's probably a bit lower than your normal speaking voice because it is more relaxed. You want to use different pitches as you speak, but you want to be in control. You don't want to be the slave of tension. A relaxed voice has a greater chance of being flexible, but a tense voice will never discover all the subtle shadings and nuances in your carefully crafted words.

Inflection — put curves on your words, letting your voice rise and fall in order to give words all the color and resonance they naturally possess. Inflection is what you do with pitch. A flat voice is like a potbellied barge that plows ahead, unaffected by and insensitive to the rise and fall of the waves around it. A flexible voice is more like a rubber raft as it yields to the contour of each wave. Riding on a barge is boring, but riding on a raft is an adventure. A story well told should be an adventure in listening as well as in telling. Each word of your manuscript, and especially the verbs and nouns, are like waves. No two are exactly alike; each has its own form. The flexible voice will yield to the individual form of each word — sometimes gentle, then powerful; high, then low.

A flat voice is not only boring but dangerous. Speaking in a monotone can damage your vocal folds as they vibrate in the same spot repeatedly. Prolonging the same tone or rate of speaking reduces the natural lubrication of the vocal folds. This has the same effect as if you rubbed your fingers together over and over again until you formed a blister. If a blister forms on your vocal folds, you will not be able to speak because of the pain. Such a condition will lead to probable surgery and a fairly extended recovery time. It seems God puts a penalty on boring people! Speaking with wide variety in rate, pitch, and volume provides natural lubrication to the vocal folds. Variety is the spice that will add life to any story you tell.

I've heard it's good to drink something warm before speaking. True?

A traditional drink of hot tea with lemon and honey has been a favorite for years. It can help relax the vocal folds and is especially inviting in cold weather. By the way, when you find yourself in a cold spell, dress warmly, especially around the throat. Wear a scarf and breathe through your nose. This will warm and slightly moisten the cold air before it slams into your vocal folds.

What kind of physical or vocal warm-up should I do before I tell the story?

You can warm up physically by stretching. The goal of stretching is relaxation, and the secret to relaxation is the creation of tension followed by its release. That's what happens when you stretch after awakening, for example. So, stretch your whole body: go up on tiptoe and try to touch the ceiling. Then jog in place for one minute. Consider yourself warmed!

To warm up vocally, begin by simply adding a vocalized yawn to your stretch as described above. Once you have yawned (you can't fake the vocal part of the yawn—it has to be legitimate), hum some five-tone scales, progressing up by a half step on each scale. Next, sing some scales on Me ("may"), Mi ("me"), Ma ("mah"), Mo ("moe"), and Mu ("moo").

Another vocal exercise you might try is called "climbing the mountain." You begin in subvocalization (an irregular, staccato sound made by allowing very little air to pass over the vocal folds as you exhale slowing, saying "ah-h-h-h"); now slide up through vocalization (your normal speaking tone, with a relaxed "ah-h-h-h," still exhaling slowly); slide further up into falsetto (the highest tone you can produce comfortably); and then back down through vocalization and ending in subvocalization. This exercise stretches your vocal folds and warms them up for maximum flexibility.

You've done it! You've mastered the story and the storyteller. You have seen the event, practically lived it over again from inside the skin of one of those present when it happened. It has become real to you. Now you are ready to share that reality with an audience.

SIX

The Fourth "R" of Storytelling: Relating

I think I have stage fright. How do I get over it?

Remind yourself of whose story this really is. The best way to remind yourself of God's ownership of the story is through prayer. All the warm-up exercises in the world will not do you as much good as prayer. Why? Because warm-ups focus on you, while prayer concentrates on God.

We have found it helpful to combine prayer with our warm-up exercises. As we do our stretching we say a silent prayer along the lines of, "Father, thank You for the opportunity to share Your message in this way. I know this is Your story. I ask Your blessing on that which You already own. Work through me, Father, that those who hear might come to know You and love You more deeply." This little prayer reminds us that the spotlight is really on our Lord in this story. The pressure is off, and we are free to enjoy the privilege of telling the story.

I would feel so much more confident if I could hold the script while I tell the story. Is that OK?

The script is a crutch. As long as you have the script or notes of any kind in your hand, you will never be totally free of them. Your concentration will not be as focused on the audience since you know you can always break contact with them in order to look at the words on the page.

Holding a script also encourages sloppy preparation. You simply won't work as hard at "nailing" the story down if you know you will always be able to cheat and look at the script. What's more, the audience will be distracted by the useless prop you are holding in your hand. Remember, the words on the page are not there for their own sake. They are only the vehicles of thought. You are speaking ideas and thoughts, not just words, to an audience. Don't focus on the words as you speak, but on the ideas they express.

In oral interpretation or reader's theater, you would hold the script in your hand and read from it as you perform. Admittedly, there are are a number of guidelines that apply with equal force to both disciplines. Storytelling, however, is different.

The "rules of engagement" in storytelling are significantly augmented. For example, there is much more movement in storytelling. The focus on the audience is certainly more sustained in storytelling. To hold the script as you tell the story is to force an unnatural amalgam of two unique forms: oral interpretation and storytelling.

We challenge you to maintain the integrity and the distinctive quality of storytelling by mastering the material so that you don't have to hold the script as you tell the story. You have taken too many brave steps to take the coward's way out now. Hang in there. We encouraged you to use oral reading while you learned to engage an audience and win the freedom to think on your feet. That was a rowboat. Now you're ready for a schooner! It's time to open your storytelling sails to the wind. Time to speak from your heart.

Aye, aye, Cap'n. Just one thing. How do I get onto the platform to begin the story?

The first impression an audience will get of you is a visual one. They begin to make judgments the moment they see you. When you approach the storytelling area, take the stage. Walk confidently and briskly without hurrying to your first spot. The first thing to do is look at the audience — and smile! Let them get a look at you before you speak. Pause just a second or two before you speak, then begin your introduction.

The only time that approaching the stage tentatively is appropriate is when someone else introduces your story and you come forward in character. The mood with which you approach the stage is the mood you will begin to establish in your listeners. They will be looking subconsciously for clues and will interpret your movements whether you want them to or not. Approach slowly, with head down, and you suggest a mood of sadness, heaviness. Approach with a light, confident stride, and the mood is correspondingly buoyant. You set the tone. Remember, every movement you make and every sound you utter will either add to or detract from the overall effectiveness of your story. Make your entrance count on the plus side of the ledger.

What happens if I forget right in the middle of the story?

The question is not "if" but "when." Everyone forgets at some point. If you have memorized the fundamental points of the story and its lesson, you should be able to improvise when you lose it. The primary reason for forgetting lines (or even forgetting where you are in the story) is lack of concentration. Losing concentration becomes particularly easy when you are telling the same story for the fiftieth time — something you could perform in your sleep. And then suddenly you are staring at a brick wall and you couldn't tell that audience what day of the week it is much less remember what in the blue-eyed world the next line is.

What then?

The last thing you want to do is let your listeners know you are in trouble. Cover your tracks by repeating what you just said, if you can remember. This will often help get you back on track. If you have carefully blocked out the story, you will sometimes recall the gesture or the blocking but forget the line that goes with it! Go ahead and make the movement by faith. You will be amazed to find that making the movement will help the line come back just in the nick of time! Sounds strange, but it works — usually.

Take the time you need, but get the story line back. Finish the story even if you need to paraphrase all the rest. But let us encourage you. In our combined storytelling experience of more than 68 years, the Lord has been faithful to help us recall hundreds of stories. We have forgotten at times, but He has always allowed us to get back on track and finish well.

Is it good to ask questions of my audience in the middle of the story?

If the question serves as a transition from one part of the story to the next and is asked rhetorically, it can work effectively. For instance, "The Pharisees had challenged Jesus with a very sticky question. He was caught between a rock and a hard place. What could He say?"

On the other hand, to interrupt an exciting story in order to quiz the audience would greatly diminish the effectiveness of the story. Usually, questions of this kind are better asked after a story. Make your questions interactive. Focus on the story's lesson rather than on its details. Questions about the details (where David came from; how old Saul was when he became king; what kind of leaves were in Adam's and Eve's aprons) are easy to ask and answer because they don't require people to think — only to remember.

Get your people to think, to interact! Ask questions such as "What would you have done if you had been Adam?" "If you were 30 years old and had just been proclaimed king of a new nation, what would you do first?" "If you had been a Pharisee at the time of Jesus, what's the one question you would have asked Him?"

Of course, there are times when specific factual questions and answers are needed. But those questions must be designed to help the student discover some lesson that is relevant to the story. You might also use questions to surface parallels with other events. For example, in the story of Ahithophel's betrayal of King David in 2 Samuel 15–17, you may want to explore the parallels between Christ and David, or between Judas and Ahithophel. An exploration of these parallels will strengthen the student's appreciation for the unity of the Bible and for God as the architect of history. Such parallels may also shed some additional light on the lesson of the story.

How do I end the story and get off the platform?

After the last line of the story, pause, look at the audience (pick out an individual or two and make eye contact), bow slightly, and then walk out of the storytelling area. If you are being assisted by a host, he or she should then read the conclusion. The story is then over and you are free to ask or answer questions.

Would it be helpful to teach my students to tell stories? If so, where should I start?

The best way to learn a story is to tell it. The first step toward telling is involvement. As you tell stories, try including your students in the story. They may be camel traders, or attendants to King Abimelech, or they may be simple townsfolk watching from a distance. Choose characters appropriate to the age of

your audience. Most of the characters will do nothing, but having identities is fun for them and helps them into the story more
easily. The mere experience of standing on the stage and pretending to be someone else (even though all they do is listen)
can be a real confidence builder. Children between first and
sixth grades will respond well to this type of stage experience.
The key is first to include them in the story you are telling. The
shy students in particular will be thrilled to actually be in the
story. The more important their "parts," the more involved they
will be.

Then, when the story is finished, ask the class members how
they felt (not what they learned—that will come later) when
the boy David killed the giant. How did they feel when they first
saw Jesus alive after they had seen Him die on the cross?

If the shy class members are holding back, you might ask a
specific question such as, "Angie, did you feel sad or happy
when you saw Jesus in the story?" For the truly withdrawn child,
any answer (and certainly any question) is a good answer or
question—or at least we should try our best to find something
good in it. That's why asking how the child feels about a part of
the story is a safe, nonthreatening way to begin.

The great thing about asking a "feeling" question is that there
can be no wrong answer. At this stage of the game, the right
answer is the honest answer. Feelings are the private property of
the owner. We can praise the child for having the courage to
tell you how he or she felt. Be careful, however, about overprais-
ing the child. If you say, "That's a fantastic answer! Incredible!"
others will hold back for fear of not being able to elicit that
great a response.

The simple expression of how a child feels opens the door to
the heart and invites you in; once you enter the heart, you can
take the express elevator up to the mind where you can explore
possibilities, answer questions, present challenges to change.
The gateway to learning that lasts is through the heart.

Now recruit your students to act the story out. Make sure to
involve the shy ones too. Make it a group exercise so that the
fear of failure is calmed. If the children are of reading age, you
may wish to divide the story into parts and have each child read
an assigned role. The parables work wonderfully for this kind of
exercise. One of Reg's most exciting times with a junior high

class came when they took one quarter to produce a radio play on the Parable of the Soils.

Four students played the four different types of soil. Groups of students played birds, thorns, and seeds, and one got to be the sower. You get the picture—everyone was in on the act! On the last Sunday of the quarter, the class presented its parable to the congregation. The students all lined up in front and stood facing the audience while they played their production, complete with sound effects.

Primitive? You bet! Fun? The class had almost 100 percent attendance every Sunday of the quarter. Effective? Kids and parents alike loved it. The shy children got involved, received tons of positive reinforcement, and had a ball at the same time they were learning.

That sounds great for working with kids, but I have an adult Sunday School class that wants nothing more than to be spoon-fed.

Working with adults is much the same as working with kids. While we have never done radio plays with adults (but why not?), we have done a number of reader's theater pieces. Reader's theater is a great way to break the ice with your group, especially if you have members who tend to be loners. Reader's theater offers them the security of a script in their hands, plus a group to support them. It can be a great first step toward storytelling.

You will find people in your classes or congregations who have gifts you never dreamed they had. Many would love to participate but figure that, because they can't teach, there just isn't any room for them to minister. Balderdash! You show them. If they don't want to read, fine. Enlist some carpenters to help build a small stage. Do you have an electrician in the group? Good, you could always use some theatrical lighting to enhance your stories. What about sound? Any audio technicians out there? People who like to sew? Ladies who could provide refreshments after rehearsals? You help them plug into the world of storytelling at the level where God has gifted them. It can be a real team effort in which everyone plays a part.

Are there any other good books that would tell me more about telling stories from the Bible?

There are a number of fine books on storytelling as well as a growing library of scripts that are designed with the storyteller in mind. Please see our bibliography for a list of helpful resources.

That's it! You are on your way. May the Lord transform lives through you and your stories, but may He begin by transforming you. That's the way it usually happens with storytellers. We get the blessing first, then we get to share it with anyone who likes a story. So, welcome to the world of true imagination. Explore! Discover! Enjoy telling stories to touch the heart!

APPENDIX A

Abraham's Return from Mount Moriah
by John Reed

Introduction
We are in Abraham's spacious tent. Abraham and Isaac have just returned from Mount Moriah where God has tested Abraham. Abraham speaks to Sarah.

Monologue
Sarah, beloved of the Lord, my life and my delight! We return to you weary with these six days journey and dusty from the way, but fulfilled with joy abounding. It was indeed a strange and wonderful journey. I know from your questions when we left that you thought my mood unusual. I deemed it best to tell you only that all was well; that Isaac and I with the two young men would go to Mount Moriah and offer sacrifice and that we would return. You may remember with what emphasis I said that we would return. I could not hide the weight of my burden, nor could I conceal the fact that I believed God to return us all.

Yes, my beloved, I will tell you all. Come now, Isaac, sit here by your mother. There, rest your head upon her heart. Your journey is over and your task completed. You are as fine a son as ever graced the eyes of a thankful father.

It began, Sarah, like any other night. I felt restless in the tent, as you may recall, and went to walk under the stars. The air was calm, the orbs of night brilliant in the sky. I thought of God's promise that our seed would be as numerous as those stars, and more in number than the sands that spread beneath my feet. I walked far from the tent in my meditations. I thought of Isaac and said aloud to Jehovah, "O Eternal God, how I praise Your Name for Your faithful mercy in giving Isaac to us. I love him so. If anything were to happen to him, it would be the rending of my heart from my breast."

I thought of the riches of God's promises. Through Isaac was the seed to come. This was the very word of God. I exulted in joyous praise. Then I felt the Presence. My senses seemed about to burst beyond my brain. I knew Jehovah was near to speak and was filled with a sense of awe and anticipation. Clear came the miracle of God's voice out of the splendid stars, "Abraham."

"Yes, Lord," I cried.

Then I heard words that turned my knees to water and my spine to sand. For God said, "Take with you your only son — yes, Isaac whom you love so much — and go to the land of Moriah and sacrifice him there as a burnt offering upon one of the mountains which I'll point out to you!"

You do well to hold Isaac close to you, Sarah. But be comforted, O thou who art fairer than the dawn; have we not completed the journey and is he not safe in your arms? Yes, Sarah, your tears are welcome. Do not check them. For so I wept on that sad night.

No other word came from Jehovah. I bit my lip to see if I were indeed awake — if this were not but a dream. Then came the realization that God had surely spoken. I did not understand. The thoughts of my soul poured out like a fountain. Isaac — our own unique, beloved son; the son of promise; the son of miracle; the son of our old age. How could it be? Does God ask me to be the designer of my own sorrow?

Sarah, you know me better than any. You know the struggles of my soul — the fears that I have learned to drown in the tidal flow of faith. How I have been haunted by the tragedy of Lot's life. How I long for Ishmael to walk before God. How I wish I could rewrite the tale of sin's scarlet agony. But Sarah, there has no grief touched me as this bewildering command. See, Isaac weeps as well. How I love you, Isaac, my son. Sarah, you shall hear of a son more faithful and obedient than ever yet the world has known.

In the long watches of the night I considered the wish of God. I recalled the promise now ancient. I remembered the barren years of waiting, and our laughter of doubt when the promise was renewed. I remembered the laughter of joy when Isaac was born. The confirmation that in Isaac would the seed be called. I knew that Isaac had no wife or offspring; that if he died the promise would fail. In the darkest hour of night my meditation ended. I believed in my heart that I must sacrifice everything to this God who has never failed us; that if He wanted back what He had given; if my son must die at my own hand to please God; if his body must be consumed totally upon the altar, then I would do as He commands, even though I did not understand.

Sarah, do you see now why my hands shook as I split the wood that morning. My night of sorrow had left me weak. But my heart was strong in its resolve. And Isaac, sweet son of promise, helped me prepare for the journey.

You know of that early morning; the donkey, the two young men to help, the wood, the fire, and the knife — the knife I use only for sacrifice. I saw your eyes upon me as I took it from its place. Isaac seemed troubled by my haste and evident resolve, but silent did remain. Three days, three nights, Sarah, our son was dead in the heart of me. Only the light of faith kept me on the path.

The sun rose on the morning of the fateful day. As its earliest beams glimmered in my eyes, hope sprang upward. I knew in my soul that God could not fail. If Isaac were the one through whom the seed would come, then the seed would come through Isaac. If Isaac were to be consumed upon the altar, God — who had brought him forth from our bodies that were as good as dead — could raise him up from the ashes of the sacrifice. God's promises could not fail.

I asked the two young men to remain behind while Isaac bore the wood upon his young shoulders and I the fire and the knife. For silent minutes we labored up the steep hillside. Then Isaac questioned, "Father, here is the wood, the fire, and the knife. But where is the sacrifice?"

I replied, "Jehovah Jireh, my son, Jehovah Jireh; the Lord will provide the lamb for a burnt offering."

When we attained the top of the hill, we found a bare rock which seemed to be a natural place for an altar. We gathered the scattered stones and carefully placed rock upon rock to fashion the place for sacrifice. Isaac helped me arrange the wood and, as the last stick was in place, his eyes met mine.

I knew the moment of truth had come. With quiet voice I told Isaac the command of God and how I had come to know that, by faith, I could give everything to God. Isaac stood silent before me as I bound his hands and placed him on the altar.

Sarah, feel how strong your son's arms are. He could have forced me aside and gained his freedom. But he submitted in unquestioning obedience. I do wish that the whole world could know about his willing sacrifice — that it might be talked of wherever men draw breath in days to come. I drew the knife to quickly do what must be done.

As I raised the knife in the morning sunlight, the voice of the angel of the Lord pierced the sky, "Abraham! Abraham!"

"Here I am," I replied.

"Do not lay a hand on the boy," He said. "Do not do anything to him. Now I know that you fear God, because you have not withheld from Me your son, your only son."

Weak with immeasurable relief, I released Isaac and clasped him to my breast. I gazed into his eyes, fearful that the trauma of the test had caused a breach between us. I heard him murmur, "It was the will of God, Father. I understand."

I heard a noise in the thicket behind us and there was a choice ram caught by its horns. In grateful joy, I took the ram and made sacrifice to the Lord. As the sweet savor ascended into the heavens, a realization swept over me. This was in truth the place of God's provision.

Sarah, we never need to fear to go to the place God chooses and do what He directs us to do, for when we arrive at the place of the Lord's direction, we will find it the place of the Lord's provision.

Then the angel of the Lord called to me again from heaven a second time and said, " 'I swear by Myself,' declares the Lord, 'that because you have done this and have not withheld your son, your only son, I will surely bless you and make your descendants as numerous as the stars in the sky and as the sand on the seashore. Your descendants will take possession of the cities of their enemies, and through your offspring all nations on earth will be blessed, because you have obeyed Me.' "

As we prepared to leave that hallowed spot, I lingered to gaze around me. It was beautiful, with a view that commanded a wide sweep of valleys and hills. I felt a strange sense that somehow God would in this place provide a portion of His blessing to the world through our descendants. And now we have returned with joy.

O my beloved friend, Eliezer. Yes, our food is prepared. Isaac, have you had enough of the dried dates and figs of the trail? Come, Sarah! Come, Isaac! We will feast in the joy of the Lord's provision. Eliezer, let me tell you what this young son of mine has done.

Conclusion

From Mount Moriah at that time it would have been possible to see the hill of Calvary. Many centuries later, another Son carried the wood upon His back. It was a cross that would become the altar upon which Jesus Christ the Son of God died for your sins and for mine. As Isaac was obedient to Abraham, so was Jesus Christ obedient to His Heavenly Father. As a lamb before its shearers is silent, so He did not open His mouth in protest (see Isa. 53:7).

The mob who watched the crucifixion of Jesus Christ shouted for another miracle: "You who are going to destroy the temple and build it in three days, save Yourself! Come down from the cross, if You are the Son of God!" (Matt. 27:40) The priests and elders of Israel cried out, "He saved others but He can't save Himself! He's the King of Israel! Let Him come down now from the cross, and we will believe in Him" (Matt. 27:41-42).

But the love that Jesus had for us held Him there. Isaac could come down from his sacrificial altar but Jesus Christ would not. He willingly died there in our place, bearing our sins in His own body on the cross (see 1 Peter 2:24).

As Abraham was willing to sacrifice his son Isaac, so our Heavenly Father did not hold back His well-beloved Son. He willingly offered Him up for us all (see John 3:16). The priests and elders mocked, "He trusts in God. Let God rescue Him now if He wants Him, for He said, 'I am the Son of God' " (Matt. 27:43). The Father did not restrain the hands of those who were shearing His Son of life. Jesus Christ died that you and I might live through His perfect sacrifice for us.

APPENDIX B

Gideon
by John Reed

I have desired to speak to you because I believe I have a message you need. Your pastor tells me that just as I and my people faced awesome enemies, you are being threatened by overwhelming odds—that doubts and fears like Midianites are overrunning your land; that the "Amalekites of temptation and sin" are devastating you.

I understand that God is asking some of you to give yourselves to a great task in His service; that you are frightened and confused, saying, "I'm far too ordinary to do anything important in God's work."

Let me encourage you. I must be the original "ordinary person," and God used me. He means to use you also. My day was a very difficult time. We had been trampled down by the hordes of Midianites, Amalekites, and their eastern desert tribes. We gained victory. You will gain victory too!

The first time we were assaulted, the enemy came riding on camels. Swift as eagles they came upon us. There were so many that it seemed they were more than the sands in number. The destroyers started here in the north and swept down across the land—all the way to Gaza in the south.

The enemy came at harvesttime and bore away our grain and

livestock. We had not recovered from that crippling blow by the next year's harvest when they came again. Each year at harvest the attacks came for seven years. Do you have problems like this?

We found caves in the mountains and went into them at harvesttime. We planted patches of grain in secluded mountain areas, away from the marauding, camel-mounted killers. Together we cried out to God for relief. In response, God sent a prophet to tell us that His hand was always mighty to save; that for us to live in fear of our enemies' gods was disobedience to the revealed will of the true God.

I was hiding in a hollowed-out place in the rocks that we used for a winepress. It was at my father's hideaway on Mount Gilead. I was crouched down, beating out a few sheaves of wheat, when I glanced up and saw a man sitting under the oak tree.

He said, "The Lord is with you, O valiant warrior." I looked around to see if he could be talking to someone else. His statement amazed me. Did he think the sheaves of wheat were Midianites? I certainly didn't feel like a valiant warrior. I began to realize this was no ordinary person that spoke to me. There was an air of authority and strength about him. He was clearly not an enemy and he was certainly not one of us. I concluded that he must be a spokesman for God.

I said, "O my Lord, if the Lord is with us, why then has all this happened to us? Where are all of His miracles which our fathers told us about, saying, 'Did not the Lord bring us up from Egypt?' But now the Lord has abandoned us and given us into the hand of Midian."

He ignored my complaint and, looking steadily into my eyes, he said, "Go in this your strength and deliver Israel from the hand of Midian. Have I not sent you?"

By this time I was getting frightened. He was talking like he was God Himself. He was surely making a big mistake talking to me about such an assignment. I said, "O Lord, how shall I deliver Israel? Behold, my family is least in Manasseh, and I am the youngest in my father's house."

He astounded me with his reply, "Surely, I will be with you, and you shall defeat Midian as though they were but one man."

Now I felt I must have a sign. I asked the person to stay while I cooked a young goat, some unleavened bread, and broth. He had me place the bread and meat on a rock and pour the broth over it.

Then he touched the food with his staff. Fire leaped out of the rock and devoured it. I knew then that it was the angel of the Lord. I thought I must die, but he told me not to fear, and disappeared. I built an altar and worshipped God there.

I had much to think about. I was just an ordinary man — Gideon, son of Joash, an Abiezrite — and I was being asked to do an extraordinary exploit. What was I to do?

Then God revealed to me the first step. My father's idols must be destroyed and an altar to God built in their place. I was fearful of my father's household and the men of the city; so, late that night when all were asleep, the altar of Baal was pulled down and the iniquitous Asherah was chopped to pieces. The altar was prepared. The wood of the Asherah was placed on the altar and I offered a bullock.

I didn't sleep very well in what was left of that night. In the morning, when my work was discovered, there arose a great clamor. Soon I was pointed out as the culprit. The people cried for my blood. But my father Joash said, "Gideon cut down Baal's altar; let Baal contend with him."

Then they called me Jerubbaal, that is to say, "Let Baal contend against him," because I had torn down his altar. As you can see, Baal has been slow to act.

With the sin of my household cleansed, I felt the sweeping of God's Spirit over me. What a revelation! What new power, energy, and assurance! If some of you lack the Spirit's fullness in your life, perhaps you need to tear down some idols and build altars where they have been.

Then all the Midianites and the Amalekites and the tribes of the eastern desert came into the land. I sounded the trumpet and summoned my brethren from Manasseh, Asher, Zebulun, and Naphtali. They came. I cried out to them, "God has called me to be your deliverer!"

They just looked at me! I could see they needed proof that God was with me in this venture. That night I prayed before them, "O Lord, if You wilt deliver Israel through me, as You have said, behold I will put a fleece on the threshing floor. If there is dew on the fleece only and not on the threshing floor, then I will know that You will deliver Israel through me, as You have spoken."

I didn't sleep very well that night either. But in the morning the ground was dry and from the fleece I squeezed a bowlful of water.

The elders' eyes widened, but I could see they needed more evidence. That night I said to God before the elders, "O Lord, please don't be angry if I speak to You again. I would like one more test with the fleece. Let the fleece be dry in the morning and let there be dew on all the ground."

That night I slept much better. In the morning, behold, the threshing floor was wet with dew and the fleece dry as a desert. The army was with me!

But I had a second lesson to learn. I looked at my 32,000 troops. They were ragged, rusty, ill-armed, but I was not bothered to be outnumbered by the enemy's 135,000. I felt that in the power of God's Spirit, I could kill a thousand by myself. Then God spoke, "Gideon."

"Yes, Lord."

"You have too many troops."

"Too many, Lord?"

"Yes. If I give Midian into your hands, you will boast and say that you have done it in your own power. Tell all those that are fearful and trembling to go home."

Most didn't share any enthusiasm about engaging the hoards of camel-riding Midianites and Amalekites. Twenty-two thousand went home, but ten thousand remained. They were the best. My heart swelled with pride as I realized their raw courage.

God had the answer for my pride. He had a final test. I was to take them down to the water and separate them on the basis of how they drank. Most knelt and drank directly from the water as fearless warriors. The others squatted down and lifted the water to their mouths with their hands and lapped like a dog laps. All the time they were glancing around as if the Midianites were about to leap on them from a bush. I was glad there were only 300 of these scared rabbits. They should have gone home when they had the chance.

God said, "With the 300, I will deliver the Midianites into your hands." I realized that to gain victory, not only must there be the purification that results in the filling of the Spirit, but the victory must be won in the power of God's Spirit without the arm of the flesh.

That night God spoke again, "Gideon."

"Oh no, Lord! Not by myself!"

But God was prepared to strengthen me by having me visit the camp of the enemy under the cover of night. I took with me Purah, my trusted servant, and crept among the tents. We overheard a man relating a dream that he had just had. "I dreamed that a loaf of barley bread tumbled into our camp. It came to my tent, turned it upside down, and knocked it flat."

Another voice said, "It is nothing less than the sword of Gideon, the son of Joash. God has given Midian and all the camp into his hand."

I bowed in thankful worship to God. We returned to our camp, divided the men into three groups of 100 each, and surrounded the Midianites' camp. Each had a trumpet and a torch covered with a clay pitcher. When I gave the signal, we broke the pitchers. As the torchlight flooded the camp, we blew our 300 trumpets. Then we shouted, "A sword for the Lord and for Gideon!"

You never saw such a sight. Some of them came right through their tent wall with their swords flailing. The Lord turned them one against another so that they slew each other while we provided the light and the music. The demoralized army fled from the scene. I alerted the soldiers that had gone home and they met the Midianites as they fled. I also summoned the men of Ephraim to the south. They slaughtered those that got through our fighting ranks. It was a great victory in all Israel that night.

Now that's a ripping good story, isn't it? People have loved to repeat it down through the years. But most are content to stop right there and they forget the third great lesson that I had to learn. It is true that purity brings Spirit-filling, and victory comes from full trust in God and not in self. But that terrible third lesson . . .

It started this way. The Ephraimites had captured and killed Oreb and Zeeb, the two Midianite chieftains. The Ephraimites came to me carrying the heads of the two kings and complained because I had not sent them word of my plan earlier. I said to them, "What have I now done in comparison with what you have accomplished? You have achieved far better glory than I. Why are the heads of Oreb and Zeeb in your hands? What I have done is merely nothing."

They cooled right down. I said to myself, *Gideon, you handled that well.* The men of Israel begged me to become their king. I cried, "I will not rule over you, nor shall my sons rule over you. The Lord shall be your ruler."

They seemed so disappointed that I thought to myself, *Surely there is something I can let them do for me.* Then I remembered that all the enemy soldiers wore earrings because they were Ishmaelites. I requested a gold earring from each of them. With the gold I made an ephod and placed it in my city, Ophrah. It was a mistake. All Israel came before it, and the worship soon degraded into Canaanite sensual practices. I did nothing to stop it.

I do not have the heart to tell you of my seventy sons and their terrible fate. You may read the account in the record of the Judges. What's that you say — seventy sons must have been a great task for my wife? I had many wives. Oh! Was that ever a mistake!

What was the third lesson? Just this. I had learned that cleansing from sin brought the power of God's Spirit and that I must depend on His hand alone in victory over enemies. What I came to know is that purity and spiritual power must be maintained. One must walk with God day by day all the way to the end. I was a good starter but a poor finisher. Far too self-assured, I had bypassed God's tabernacle and priesthood. Weak and wayward as they had become, still I should have used the gold to restore them.

I had forgotten to talk with God about the problems of my life. Somehow it seemed that God was only necessary in an emergency. At other times I could trust my own wisdom. Ordinary men can handle ordinary days. But I needed God as much in times of peace as I did in wartime. With Satan ready to ruin us at any time, there are no ordinary days.

It is true that my land was undisturbed for 40 years. But after God had given us such a great slaughter of our enemies, do you know how long it takes to raise up a new generation of warriors? It takes 40 years. You see, all the credit belongs to God.

Whatever you do, when you make a good start, stay with it to the end. God can take ordinary people and do great exploits. The "Midianites of doubt and fear" can be slain. The "Amalekites of temptation and sin" can be destroyed. But it is so easy to get into a religious routine and forget that total victory comes only by God's grace. Rise up! Destroy your idols! In the fullness of the Spirit, trust God to work a resounding victory for you in days of crises and in days of peace.

(Biblical quotations based on the *New American Standard Version*.)

APPENDIX C

The Goblet and the Grail
by Reg Grant

So, this is what Christians look like. I've often wondered — wondered what you would think of me and how you were getting on. Not too well, by the looks of it. But if there's one thing I've learned, you don't judge a book by its cover. And you never take fruit from strangers. My name is Adam, the first man. I've come to tell you a story. You may learn a secret or two along the way; many of my children have. Especially about . . . I'll let you discover that for yourselves. Very well. The story of "The Goblet and the Grail."

In the beginning, there was nothing to forgive. We saw eye to eye on nearly everything. I did not yield to her. She did not bow to me. She was my helper as God is my helper — the one who makes up for what is lacking in me. Now we are different. Now there's something to forgive.

More than anything I wanted to please her. She was, in a word, perfect. Queen of all creation — the most stunning creature — there are none in your world to compare with Eve. The sun paled in the light of her intellect. She had an amazing ability to interpret new information. Give that woman time to think and she could figure anything out. Soft as rain, she was. Of course, I didn't know what rain was at the time. But I felt that rain would come one day, whatever it was, and that somehow Eve would be the cause of it, as she was the cause of everything that fascinated or bewildered me.

It really didn't amount to much — the act itself, I mean. It didn't take much time or strength to move a world away from God. In fact, it took a great weakness. Mine was no heroic act, but the act of a coward. Every act of disobedience against God is ultimately an act of cowardice. Only the coward knows what it means to shift his allegiance in the middle of a fight. Though it wasn't much of a fight. Eve didn't have time to think (which was a problem) and I did (which was a problem).

It all happened so quickly, with such lethal detachment. Sin did not come screaming into our garden on fiery wings. No, sin is rarely as obvious as that. It was more like a well-intentioned friend. He visits with you over coffee, suggesting — only suggesting — but with a casual urgency in his voice, that you commit a minor indiscretion for the sake of a greater good — the greater good being whatever you want.

Sin came sheathed in subtlety. We stood naked before him. He came coiling, twisting, wrapping the word of God in a delicious lie. He promised wisdom; he promised the world; he promised we would become like God.

I knew something was wrong. I found Eve sitting beneath the tree. She was staring at her hands — rubbing them as if she were trying to remove a stain. "Eve? Eve."

I knew what had happened. She wouldn't look at me. She held out her hand with the fruit. My Eve. She was the only woman in the world. But if the world had been filled with women, she would still have been the only woman in the world for me. I remember how strange it felt even to think of doing it — disobeying. But I stood to lose so much. In that short space of time — just enough time to doubt — I felt the garden become a prison, and God had locked me in.

He mocked me, denying me what I wanted most. So we took the cup of the serpent. A goblet of poison that went down as smooth as nectar. We disobeyed and became very unlike God. We began to die. Immediately we were cut off from each other, cut off from joy, cut off from God.

Shame rushed over us. We sewed clumsy aprons of leaves — I suppose in a desperate attempt to regain some of the dignity we had sold for a piece of fruit, a slice of independence. The awful thing is, I have never known a day's freedom since I first acted independently from God. Independence from God brings bondage, not freedom; sorrow, not joy. And worst of all, fear — fear of His judgment.

We ran. Ran to the trees. Stupid. Running from God is like trying to run from yourself. No matter how far you go, He's always there.

He knew what we had done, and yet He asked. He was giving us an opportunity to confess. There was a sadness in our Lord's eyes, as if He were feeling the pain of a thousand thousand souls, not just two. He is a compassionate Judge. Even in His curse, He blessed us with the promise of One who would destroy our enemy. Somehow this deliverer, this great warrior would come through the seed of the woman. She would become the mother of the living through Him, not the mother of death. So, by faith I named her Eve, mother of all living.

The Lord brought us the skin of an animal to replace the work of our own hands. The world outside was no Eden. Those skins protected us and, at the same time, reminded us of our sin. I wish I could live that day over again. I wish it every day of my life — and I have lived a long time. Death came slowly for us. Not slowly enough for others.

On still summer nights late in my life, I remember hearing his voice calling from the fields — crying from the ground. Abel — his name means "breath." And so was his life — a breath — here and then a wicked man killed him in the field — who knows why. But God is good; He gave us Seth. We have enjoyed Seth and his brothers and sisters. But it was never like Eden, never like it was intended to be.

At first I wanted to get back in. I felt that if I worked hard enough, looked long enough, I could find a breach in the wall that separated me from paradise.

But there was more to it than mere physical separation from the tree of life. There was more than a wall around Eden. There was a wall between God and me. Sin had shut me out of the garden. No, I had shut myself out. Sin was just the key.

It's so sad. I convinced myself I would be unlocking the secret door of knowledge. But I found out — sin isn't a key to freedom. Oh, sin will unlock a lot of doors, but the doors never lead to freedom — only to bondage. And every door you walk through — every sin; every lie; every lustful glance; every itching little hate; every selfish, grasping twitch — takes you deeper and deeper into prison.

Until, somewhere near the end of your life, you come to a black door — only you can't tell it's black, because you left the light a long time ago. Everything is black now, but you haven't noticed — the change has been so gradual, the way so smooth, the descent to the gates of hell so comfortable. No, this is like every other door, every other sin you've walked into by your own will.

It's hot here. You are thirsty. The key will unlock the door. There's a goblet waiting on the other side, filled to the brim with the same old poison. You're addicted now. It doesn't satisfy — only creates a craving for more. And all you can think is, *Get through the door; taste the sin one more time.* And you think you hear laughter coming from the other side. But it's the kind of laughter that springs from the throat of death, a laughter of madness and pain and a shared horror. And somehow you wonder if this is the last door, the last chance you will have to turn back.

As the key scrapes in the lock, a dismal light washes the door. You detect names scratched into the metal, of those who had gone before, the defiant ones who screamed, "I am free" in the midst of the prison. And the longer you look, the more names you see. Hundreds of names, thousands, tens of thousands of names. And there, just over the keyhole, as the key twists, an unseen hand begins to scratch your name from the other side of the door — scratching through the black metal of the last door.

Don't turn the key. Don't sin, because you never know which door might be the last.

All those names on hell's door — they're my children, you know. All mine. Your name hasn't been scratched into the door yet. It may be written in a different place. It may be written in a Book of Life, not on death's door. It may be inscribed with the blood of a Lamb slain from the foundation of the world, not chiseled into an eternal gravestone. I don't know.

But I do know you have a choice. You may choose to follow me and my example. You may take up the key of sin and open as many doors as you dare. See how far you can go, how many goblets of poison you can swallow and get away with it. Follow me in my rebellion — in my declaration of independence from God — and sweat out the rest of your years, trying to convince yourself that God likes what He sees. Make no mistake. It's not His image in us that He condemns. It's what we've done with His image.

I was created from the dust of the ground, with a brain. I could think, reason, integrate knowledge and life. That I took eagerly. He gave me a heart. I could feel. That I took joyfully. And He gave me a will — the freedom to choose. There have been many times I wished I could give it back, that He would do the choosing for me.

But that wouldn't work. God refuses to force His love on an unwilling subject. I had to choose Him freely, or not at all. I — we are all — made in His image, though it's harder to recognize now.

Trying to see the image of God in man is too often like trying to identify someone by looking through the wrong end of a telescope on a foggy day. Sin does that. It obscures our spiritual vision, our ability to recognize the image of God in man. But it's still there, and no one saw it more clearly than Jesus. The image had been marred. Fellowship had been broken. And Jesus was the only one who could restore the relationship between God and man on a permanent basis.

So He took on my image. Not that He ever sinned — He could not — but He took on the form of a sinful man, took my sins on Himself — mine and yours — all of them. He died in our place. And His Father let Him do it. Can you imagine loving something you made so much you would let your son die to get it back? That's how much God loves us. That's how much He loves you.

Death is conquered. Jesus, the second Adam, did it. He rose from the dead. You never have to die. Not real death, not spiritual death. Oh, you might pass out of that body into a far greater one — pass out of this world of shadows into a world of true color and light beyond your imagining to see Him as He is. But that's hardly something to be feared, is it? If you are a Christian, the death of your body is a mere waking from what you will come to regard as a rather fitful dream. If you're not a Christian, this fitful dream is only a prelude to one hell of a nightmare.

Don't make the same mistake I made. I was young — 24, 25 hours old. I figured wherever Eve was, there was Eden — very romantic, I thought at the time. But I was wrong. There's nothing romantic in becoming a corpse, not even if you're holding hands. Wherever God is, there is Eden. We no longer have to hide.

Put your trust in the second Adam, Jesus Christ. I took the goblet from the serpent. I took it for my own sake. I swallowed death and you all died. Jesus took the goblet from His Father. He knelt in a different garden and prayed, "Father, if it is possible, let this cup

105

pass from me." Nevertheless, He took it for your sake. He swallowed death that you may live — drank it down in one bitter gulp, so you won't have to taste it.

Now the Lord Jesus offers you another cup. No ordinary goblet, but a grail filled with His lifeblood. It's the only antidote to the poison. There is no other remedy.

Were you to liquify the best of your works — were you by some dark alchemy able to condense the noblest desires of the greatest men who ever lived, and drink it down — that distilled goodness would only add a flower to the mound above your grave. Only the blood of Jesus Christ can save you from eternal death.

I've wanted to say something for a long time: I'm sorry. I've never been able to tell you, my children — I'm sorry. Can you forgive me? Can you forgive your father? I hope so. You will never be more like our Lord than when you forgive me, because I caused all your pain. I am responsible for every baby's death, for every smoking gun, for every tear. For every lash of the whip, for every thorn, for every blow of the hammer on the nail.

And if He forgave me who caused all your pain, He can forgive you who suffer because of me. You can't make up for the sins you have committed against Him any more than I could. It's all fig leaves. All you can do is drink His cup — His grail.

Believe the God-Man Jesus died in your place on the cross, was buried, and that He rose from the dead three days later. He wants to forgive you, to make a new creation out of you, to offer you life for all eternity, but only on His terms. It's a very exclusive arrangement, I know. But then so is death.

It's your choice. Death or life? The goblet or the grail?

APPENDIX D

A Shepherd's Song
by John Reed

It is very gracious of you to allow a shepherd to come into your presence. Shepherds do not have an honored position in society. The only ones lower than we shepherds are the lepers. We have a reputation for being treacherous — that sometimes we think "what is thine is also mine." But that's only true for some few of us. And those few put the rest of us in a bad light. The biggest problem with shepherds is the fact that . . . well, there's an old saying among us that "he who walks where the sheep walk has difficulty keeping his feet clean." We don't get a chance to wash very often. If you are going to be a Hebrew, respected and honored, you have to wash very often.

The experience that I would like to tell you about took place in the winter. I was among those shepherds who watched the flock at Migdal Eder.

My name is Heber. I am a shepherd on the night watch. In the midst of the field where my flock is located there is a tower. That is how my field got its name, for Migdal Eder means "the tower of the flock."

When you come to the field of Bethlehem where the flocks are, the first thing you notice is the tower on which I now stand. It's a stone tower — round, about 10 feet high and 10 feet across.

Around the top of the tower there is a low wall. Around the out-side of the tower winds a stairway.

I am here on the top of the tower tonight with my beloved shepherd friend Nathan. Nathan has been here for much longer than I. I've only been with the night shepherds for a short time. I had watched the flocks during the day, but it was about two months ago that my honored father died and was buried. Now I have his position.

I grieve deeply for the loss of my father. He always loved to watch the flock at night, especially so that he might be with Nathan, for Nathan knows the Scriptures well. They loved to sit by the fire here on the tower and talk of the ancient prophecies and Scriptures of Israel.

You are probably surprised that shepherds would know anything about the Scriptures. We are trained very carefully at the knees of our mothers and fathers. I'm sure that shepherds don't know as much as the people in Jerusalem or even the people of Bethlehem. But those things that we do know, we have time to think about.

On this particular night it is very dark. The light from the fire shines only a few feet out from the tower. If you could see all the way out to the surrounding flock, you would see two or three hundred sheep assembled around the tower.

If you listen carefully, you will hear the shepherd's pipes. You will hear the flute-like music as it drifts across the flock from one side. Listen — do you hear a similar tune coming in from the other side? Out there is Benjamin, and over there is Eliezer, our fellow shepherds. Their music keeps the flock rested and at peace during the night.

Soon Benjamin and Eliezer will mount the steps and come to the top of the tower. Then it will be time for Nathan and me to take the pipes and soothe the sheep. We will also take our shepherd's staff and our slings. You see, these are the fields where the young shepherd boy, David, killed his lion and his bear. The lions and the bears are still out there and now we must watch for them.

If you know Jewish custom, and especially if you have read carefully the Mishnah, which is our record of the ceremonial responsibilities of the Jews, you might be a little surprised that there is a flock so near to the town. It is less than a mile from Bethlehem, on the way to Jerusalem. While Bethlehem is a small city, it is unusual to have flocks this close. The Mishnah requires that the flocks be kept in the wilderness. Why is this one so close? There is good reason. This is the flock that keeps the sacrificial animals for the temple in Jerusalem. It is here that servants come from the temple and take from among these choice sheep the animals for the daily sacrifices. This has been the depository for the sacrificial animals for centuries now.

Tonight Nathan reminds me, "Heber, in this city of Bethlehem the ancient prophets foretell that the Messiah, the Prince of God, the coming King and deliverer of Israel, will be born." That doesn't impress me a great deal; that promise has been made for many generations — although I remember, as Nathan tells me this, that it did impress my father greatly. As Nathan is talking, the fire burns brightly, we hear the shepherd's pipes and the low bleating of the flock.

Suddenly, suddenly as if by magic, the darkness is turned into blazing light. As our eyes become accustomed to the light, we see before us, on the wall of the tower, an apparition, a creature, something I've never in my life seen. And I'm struck with terrible fear, and Nathan is struck with fear as well, and fear changes to awe.

Then that something, whatever it is, speaks and says, "Fear not," and my fear is eased; and I comprehend by a sweeping of God's Spirit Himself the realization that I am in the presence of an angel.

He speaks, "Fear not: for, behold, I bring you glad tidings of great joy, which shall be to all people. For unto you is born this day in the city of David, a Saviour, which is Christ the Lord."

And as he speaks, Benjamin and Eliezer come running up the steps. They too stand in the presence of this mighty angel. The angel speaks again and says, "And this shall be a sign unto you; Ye shall find the babe wrapped in swaddling clothes, lying in a manger."

As he speaks, suddenly the whole sky is filled with angels, from horizon to horizon, as far as the eye can see — thousands upon thousands of angels saying, "Glory to God in the highest, and on earth peace, good will toward men." Then the angel and the other angels seem just to rise up into the sky and are gone.

I suppose that the whole experience took no more than a half a minute, or a minute at the most. And so filled with awe, amazement, and confusion am I . . . that I thought . . . I must have dreamed. But I do not ever recall four men in one place having the same dream at the same time.

And Nathan — how good it is to have Nathan with us at a time like this; for there is in his maturity a serenity and strength, and he assures us that we are to make our way immediately to Bethlehem. So down the tower we go. We run across the fields together, the four of us, leaping over the low walls that stand in our way.

When we come into Bethlehem, we see the small town as we've never seen it before. There are obviously many people here. We agree that the most likely manger in all of the town of Bethlehem is at the inn.

The inn looks like a huge stone fort. There are four walls surrounding a large courtyard. Inside these walls there are small, cubicle-like rooms that make up the rooms of the inn. Looking through the door to the inn, we can see that some of the doors to the rooms have canvas or blankets of skin draped over them; some are just open. It is obvious that there are people in all of them. In the courtyard there are a few goats staked out with a little food before them. By the fire there are three men squatting, drinking, and talking with one another.

We move quickly to the side of the inn where the lean-to stable stands against the wall. It has a thatched roof and outer stone wall. A canvas hangs over the opening. We approach, holding the canvas aside.

Down toward the center of the line of animals we see a single flame from a lamp on a stone ledge. A man is standing there, and between us and him there are several donkeys and oxen. It's easy to see that beyond him there are more animals. As we come through the opening the man raises his hand, as if to tell us to be silent. He comes toward us and says, "What do you wish?"

We explain what had happened on the hillside; about the angels and all that we saw on that glorious night; that the angel told us that here in this place the Messiah had been born.

He says, "I am Joseph; and it is true, for just as angels appeared to you, so an angel appeared to me and to my wife Mary." Then he says, "His name is Jesus. Come and see."

And as we come, I realize that on this cold night, the stable with its many animals may be the warmest place in all of Bethlehem. We see the baby lying in the cattle-feeding trough, the manger.

I look at the baby with its tiny arms and legs individually

wrapped according to our custom of swaddling — wrapped so that his arms and legs would be straight. When I see him wrapped this way, my mind plunges back those several weeks to when I saw my father wrapped so very similar to that. But for the fact that my father's body was wrapped also with myrrh and aloes and other spices, you would have said that this little infant was wrapped for his burial.

But this is no time for such thoughts. The Messiah is born — the future King of Israel, the deliverer has come. We recount to his mother those experiences on the hillside — how the angel came and the angel chorus sang. We are thrilled in the repetition of that message.

I look carefully at his mother and am struck with her beauty. She has dark hair and eyes. She seems almost fragile, tiny, too soft for such a hard experience as this. She only listens and doesn't say a word.

In Israel, if you have money and are expecting a child, you hire musicians. The musicians come outside your house, and when the news comes that a son is born, the musicians play and there is great rejoicing that a male child is born.

I whisper to Nathan, "How unfortunate that Joseph and Mary are here with the greatest and most glorious male child ever born in the history of the world and there are no musicians to celebrate. There are no minstrels to sing."

And Nathan, in his characteristic way, slips his arm around my shoulder and says, "Heber, this Son is honored indeed, for his Father sent the minstrels from heaven to celebrate His birth."

Then I remember the angel chorus and I have to admit that there hasn't been a Jewish father in all the history of the world that has ever celebrated his son's birth quite so appropriately.

As we leave the stable, we are filled with anticipation and joy that the Messiah is born. We hurry to the front of the inn and come in through the door. The men are still there by the fire. I feel great joy in my heart that they haven't gone to bed. We go to them and tell them all that has happened. They don't seem to share the enthusiasm that we feel. Yet they listen and I can tell that they are thinking deeply.

As we make our way back across the fields, we sing praises to God. Our lips say things that we have never said before in our lives. We express our praise, joy, and gratitude to the eternal Father that the deliverer, redeemer, the Saviour, the King of Israel has come — that soon the yoke of Rome will be broken and we will be free.

The sheep are still there. I don't know whether some angels had been sent to take care of them in our absence or not. I hadn't thought about the sheep from the moment the angel had appeared until this particular moment when we return.

The years that follow are long years. We never see Jesus again. We want to, but shepherds are very confined. The sheep are always here and need us. Regularly from the temple in Jerusalem come the servants of the priest to get the sacrificial sheep, and as they come, we ask them about news of the Messiah. But there is nothing.

Many years pass and I grow older, and Nathan becomes so feeble that he has to be carried up the steps. But still he keeps coming. Then we hear that there is out in the wilderness a prophet, speaking like Elijah of old, calling the nation to repentance. My heart leaps within me and I cry, "It is He; it is the Messiah."

But Nathan says, "No, Heber, it is not the Messiah, for this man's name is John, and Joseph told us the Messiah's name is Jesus."

Soon we hear that this John has baptized Jesus, the Messiah, in the Jordan River. The temple servant says, "John proclaimed that Jesus was the Lamb of God that takes away the sin of the world."

I must admit: that was a shock. We shepherds don't have much to be proud of. But we have been proud about Jacob telling us that God was the shepherd of Israel. David called the Lord his shepherd. We envisioned the Messiah as a shepherd, but now John is saying that He is a sacrificial lamb? A lamb like the lambs that surround the tower? We don't understand.

Then the news comes in like a flood. The news of His ministry throughout the land of Israel. Miracle after miracle is performed. Many people flock to follow Him. We feel a sense of eager anticipation.

But then the word comes that He has been betrayed, that the priests have taken Him, that He has gone to a trial, that He has been crucified. The Messiah crucified? Laid in a tomb? I am bewildered, confused, and very sad. It seems that the hope of Israel has gone to the grave with Jesus.

But ancient Nathan comforts me and says, "Ah, Heber,

remember — when God makes a promise, God will keep it, even though we do not know the way."

Then a man named Prochorus comes from Jerusalem. He says that he is one of the deacons of the newly formed church there. He had heard about us from the temple servant and has come to ask us about what happened that night so long ago. He tells us that Jesus is alive from the dead, that He has ascended on a cloud and gone to the right hand of the Lord God! Not only that, but He had promised to return in the same manner to bring redemption to Israel! That is very good news!

I'm a man of the outdoors. I saw Him when He came the first time, and I must confess that now I rarely see a cloud, but that I expect Him to be on it.

Perhaps the biggest moment of all, since that moment when the angel came that night so long ago, is when Prochorus brings to us Luke, the doctor. Dr. Luke asks us to repeat in detail the things that happened to us on that night. He seems intensely interested in it and has us go over it again and again. He tells us that he is writing an account of the life of Jesus for a friend.

He explains to us that the Messiah was in truth God's sacrificial lamb, that Christ died for the sins of all men, and that all who believe this and believe that Christ is alive from the dead will have eternal life given to them. He says, "Heber, just believe in Him and God will forgive your sins, because Jesus has died for them. He will grant you eternal life."

I believe — put my trust in Him — and joy floods my heart. I quickly go to Nathan and tell him. He also becomes a believer. Yet, something troubles me and I finally find the courage to ask, "Dr. Luke, something has bothered me for many years. Why do you think it was that the angels came to us lowly shepherds? Why didn't they appear to the priests or at least the scribes and Pharisees?"

The good doctor thinks for a moment and then says, "Why, Heber, surely the answer is in the message that the angels gave. They proclaimed that the good news was for all men. They were saying that everyone — from the lowest to the highest — needs and can have this wonderful Saviour."

I see how true that is. But I am concerned that I had puzzled over it for more than three decades while Luke understood it right away. Perhaps that's why he's a doctor and I'm a shepherd.

Now I gladly share that message with all who come near me: "Christ died for you whether you are rich or poor, wise or ignorant, washed or unwashed. You need Him. He died and rose again for your salvation. If you have never believed in the Lord Jesus Christ, will you do so right now?"

APPENDIX E

Something to Steal
by Reg Grant

Introduction #1

What drives a man? Motivates him? Compels him to choose the bad rather than the good, hell rather than heaven? Why do some men conspire against their own joy by rejecting the source of all joy in Jesus Christ? Of course, most do not reject outright. They merely postpone their decision until it's too late — but the results are the same. The door is left open a crack, but they rarely look through to see the suffering of the Saviour for them. This is the story of a man who almost waited too long to look — a thief for whom God's gift had become "something to steal."

Introduction #2

The Christmas season is upon us — with all its magic and wonder, its colored lights and gift-giving. A busy time, but also a time for reflection. If you listen closely, you can still hear the angel's voice: "I bring you good news of a great joy which shall be for all the people; for today in the city of David there has been born for you a Saviour who is Christ the Lord." That simple message says one thing: There is a gift waiting for you and for all men. It is a gift for bankers and beggars, for kings and cripples, and shepherds watching over their flocks by night. It is even a gift for thieves.

Some receive it gladly; others mock all giving. But for one thief in particular — one who stole from those whom Jesus blessed — the gift of God's love becomes "something to steal."

[Half sung, half spoken; dirgelike]

My life was a burden to me,
But now I depart with a cry —

[Speaker is interrupted by the sound of approaching footsteps.]

Sh-h-h.

No, it's not time yet. Silas? Why did the guards let you in? Why have you come? To see me off? Or to hear one more story from "the poet"? I'm not much in the mood for fairy tales. I guess I should thank you for coming. What shall we talk about? Fishing? Or the judgement of God on Rome? On me? The judgement of God — on me. Yes, a story is in order here — a true one, though its meaning is lost to me. Perhaps the answer lies in the telling. Very well . . . for you, Silas, and for you, my fellow-prisoners — the all-too-brief story of "the poet."

My, was it that long ago? The world was a fairy tale then, and I was cast as the child beggar and thief. The sun was a burning eye that hung so long suspended in midair, revealing my misdemeanors. But the night — the night had a billion sparkling eyes that witnessed my crimes and never told. The night could keep a secret. And so I loved the darkness more than the light. It's where I learned to survive. My parents had died the year before, so I had taken to the streets to steal and beg whatever I could to get by. It was in my twelfth year. . . .

Winter sprang like a lion from under the leafy quilt of autumn, biting at my bare toes, at my ears and eyelashes and my nose. I remember one night in particular. The wind was shrieky and cold and the clouds sailed by the moon on the crest of that chilling gale in search of a warm and cozy harbor away from the threat of the storm. Through the racing clouds I could see the stars twinkling so brightly, I could almost hear them sing. No storm could muffle their glittering anthem, though the clouds came like an advancing army, tumbling one on top of the other until the dusty streets of Bethlehem became a patchwork quilt of black and midnight blue. The heavens and the earth were at war that night. . . .

And I was caught in the middle — hungry and alone — but I was

E

in no mood for philosophy. I was far more concerned over the
pains in my belly than the pains in my heart; and so I started to
look for an easy mark.

The crowd was ripe for the picking and, thanks to the census,
there was a bountiful harvest of pockets and purses to pluck. So
many people I have never seen in one place — like sheep before the
shearer to pay their taxes. The muffled sounds of jingling coins and
angry voices demanding a bed for the night all blended together to
compliment the howling wind and lend credence to the storm.
They were all angry. The census was hated and unnecessary, and
there were no beds to be had.

I wandered down the narrow, winding streets toward the edge of
town in the hope of finding a warm stable for the night. I had
found three drachmas lying unused in a Roman's purse — enough
for some food, but beds were selling high in Bethlehem that night.

As I rounded the corner, my eyes fixed upon the dull glow that
spilled from the doorway of Jacob's Well. It was the oldest and
cheapest tavern in Bethlehem. The wind carried the belligerent
voice of the proprietor, appropriately named Jacob, to my tired
ears. He was arguing with someone, or really *at* someone, as was
his custom.

As I approached I could see a man standing in the dim light that
fell from the main door of the tavern. Apparently, he wanted a
room like the rest. But old Jacob's face was drawn up tighter than a
Pharisee's purse. The stranger pointed behind into the darkness
and spoke lowly, but intensely.

And then I heard it — a woman's cry coming from the darkness.
The stranger was at her side immediately, but I watched Jacob. His
eyes were hidden beneath bushy brows and so his thoughts eluded
me. But I saw the crinkly, leather countenance of that old man
soften, and for an instant I saw my father's face when he put me to
bed at night. He lumbered over to the young couple and put his
rough hand on the stranger's shoulder. He pointed away along the
eastern edge of Bethlehem toward the inn.

While he talked, I made my move. I skirted to the side of the
tavern and sneaked around the corner and in the door. Old Jacob
loved his wine. He kept some of the best under the counter on a
shelf towards the back. The wine was warm and would make me
sleep. Eliphaz, Jacob's business partner, was talking to some Roman officers, and so he took little notice of me scooting behind the

counter. Ah, there it was! I grabbed the earthenware jar and was out the door like a shadow in the wind, and just in time — old Jacob was turning to come back inside.

From my hiding place, I watched as the stranger hurriedly thanked Jacob and led the donkey that carried his wife into the night. As they passed through the light I caught a glimpse of the woman's face — the girl's face — so young and pretty, with an innocence lined in pain. The donkey was bearing a double burden: a mother and her unborn child; and from the looks of things, the baby was most eager to see what the world was like. If he only knew. . . . *Why would any baby want to come into a world like this?* I thought. The wind picked up. Jacob stared after them a long time before he went back inside.

With the wine jar tucked snugly inside my cloak next to my bare chest, I made my way around the back of the tavern and set out to follow the soon-to-be parents. If there was a warm spot in Bethlehem, this man would find it.

So on we went along the edge of the city. What a monster of a night! I gulped the warm red liquid. It carried the taste of pitch but dulled the teeth of that biting wind. I heard sounds of the sheep in the fields along the road to Jerusalem — and my thoughts went to my friend Heber, standing watch in his lonely tower, watching over the sheep for sacrifice. This would be a night he and the other shepherds wouldn't soon forget.

Every once in a while, the woman would cry to her husband — Joseph, she called him. He was there, walking alongside, whispering words of love and comfort, but they didn't stop. They needed to find shelter quickly.

The wind was whipping around with a fury that I haven't seen since, and more than once I saw the woman lose her balance. A bad fall on that rocky slope could have lost the child. It was almost as if someone, or something, was trying to destroy them. But Joseph was there.

Finally, they topped the brow of the hill. There was the inn a short distance below. It reminded me of a fortress with its high, bleak walls. Joseph ran into the courtyard, calling for the innkeeper. He returned quickly, moving his donkey into the stable. At least it was dry. There was a large rock between the stable and the inn where the wind was blocked off. There I made my bed for the night. I drank the wine — and slept.

It was long into that black night that I was roused from my dreams by a baby's cry, coming from the stable. All was very still and for the moment it seemed as if that cry had stopped the world, and everything—men, animals, the earth, the stars—listened to the cry of the babe in the stable. And then a sound came from the sky away over the flocks on the north side of Bethlehem, and a light burned and then it was gone. And I felt a breeze on my cheek. The clouds had gone; the storm had passed and the night was watching the earth.

I crept around the corner of the stable and peered in at the opening. It was dark inside except for the dim glow coming from a flickering lamp. The animals were still. The mother was wrapping the new arrival in swaddling—a boy. Joseph stroked her hair and took his new infant bundled warmly against the cold and held him. They both looked at him for a long time; and then they prayed. I couldn't hear the words, but the words didn't matter.

I watched Joseph lay his son tenderly in the manger. And for the first time in my life, I wanted to give—I wanted to give this little stranger something. The feeling was hard to shake as I looked at Him in the manger. Here, I thought, we had something in common, the little stranger and I—no bed.

I couldn't sleep—too much had happened. I walked the streets till dawn. That was my first encounter with the little stranger—they named him Jesus.

I saw Caleb, the old shepherd, a few days later. He said that the night of the storm he had been on the road to Jerusalem on his way to help with the sheep. Just as he reached the tower, he said, there appeared to him and the other shepherds an angel of the Lord surrounded by sparkling light and in his eyes "golden joy." His words like honey and saffron flowed that the promised seed had come, the Messiah had been born, and they would find Him in the city of David, lying in a manger.

I had spent too many nights listening to that old shepherd's tales to fall for this one. Believe me, the play of shadow and starlight, the moaning wind, and too long alone with sheep will do more to bring on signs and wonders than anything I know.

Still, the other shepherds gave me the same story . . . and Jesus had been born that night. He was in a manger . . . so, they found their baby King bathed in straw and perfumed with the royal incense of goats and cattle and sheep. It's funny—whoever this baby was, the animals provided more of a welcome for him than the people did.

I think it was three days later that I left for Jerusalem. It was a bit more cosmopolitan: fatter people, fatter purses. I "borrowed" one last bottle of wine from old Jacob before I left, for old times' sake. I took on a partner in Jerusalem who would steal from the crowds as I told stories in the city streets. Was I a thief? It depends on your perspective, for I gave them my dreams and in my dreams, my heart — dreams spun in gold and silver. It was only fair that I should receive gold and silver in return! So my youth fled from me and close behind, my innocence.

Years later, after golden dreams had turned to rust — after I had joined the Sicarii, the assassins in an effort to rid my land of this Roman filth — I was plying my trade when I saw Him standing in the crowd — the little stranger, grown-up — Jesus. I don't know how I knew it was He. I hadn't seen Him in 33, 34 years; but He looked at me like He'd known me forever. He looked at me as if He wanted to give me something. You know, all I could think of? Whether or not my partner had tried to steal from Him. It wouldn't have done any good; He didn't have money.

But you know, Silas, I have read men's eyes all of my life and He had something that I couldn't steal — and I'm the best. I've spent the last three years trying to find out — and I still don't know — what He has. That's the puzzle.

I do know that He's a good man. He doesn't deserve the cross. I heard all the chanting for Barabbas out there early on. After they threw me in here to wait, they brought Jesus in — just before you came. I watched through the cracks in the door. I'm glad you didn't see what they did to Him. You know, I cried for the first time in 30 years. For a man I don't even know.

They almost killed Him. If I were Him, I would have begged for death — anything to avoid the cross — but He was determined to stay alive. He was in a private war against something bigger than Rome, bigger even than death — and He never cried out. "The Thief and the Stranger" . . . would make a good story — but there isn't time for that. It won't be long; you'd better go. Thank you.

[To himself]
He never cried out. He never said a word. "Like a lamb that is led to slaughter . . . so He did not open His mouth." It makes sense. . . .

[Half sung, half spoken]
My life was a burden to me,
But now I depart with a cry
The day that the stranger became my King
They hung us on crosses to die.

Conclusion #1

The voice of the thief who repented calls to us across the years. He speaks to believers and unbelievers alike. "Why wait? Why not now?" Why do some of us, we who believe, settle for lives of suspended spiritual animation? Truth without power — conscription without conviction? We have gazed on His suffering; we have looked through the crack in the door and seen an empty tomb.

God was not buried in Jerusalem. God is here. Jesus Christ our Lord is with us, in us this day. Just as real, just as powerful as when He fought against death and won. In Him we find life — abundant, rich, overflowing, eternal — and free. It can't be stolen. It's a gift.

Don't be like the thief. Don't wait. If you haven't ever trusted in our risen Lord, then trust Him to forgive you now. For those of us who know Him, let us follow Him as the wise men followed the star until they came into His presence. One day we will see Him face-to-face. We will know Him, though we have never seen Him; and He will look at us, all former thieves, as if He has known us forever.

Conclusion #2

The thief on the cross realized that the stranger possessed nothing of value. Rather, the stranger, this Jesus, was Himself the valued gift — One whose love and life cannot be stolen or earned, but only received with joy and thanksgiving.

Shall we pray? If you have never received the greatest of all Christmas gifts, then I invite you to accept God's gift of His Son tonight. He died in our place for our sins. But He rose on the third day and lives to give us eternal life. Believe in Him; trust Him; receive Him; rejoice in Him.

Father, we pray Your blessing on this assembly. We thank You for the precious gift of Your Son in whose name we pray. Amen.

CHARACTER AND SCENE ANALYSIS

Work through this outline in order to uncover and record relevant details about the character you wish to portray and how he or she fits in the scene.

I. **Title of play:**
   A. Author:
   B. Character:

II. **Analysis of Character**

   A. **"Who am I?"** Search for character's life prior to the play's beginning. (A biography including family background, environment, and so on.)
      1. What is the function of your character in the play?
      2. What characteristics or traits are most important?
      3. List all the adjectives you can think of to describe the character.

   B. **Physical Characteristics**
      1. Race
      2. Type/build
      3. Age
      4. Strength/health
      5. Carriage/movements
      6. Speech
      7. Dress

C. **Mental Characteristics**
   1. Native intelligence
   2. Thinking habits
   3. Education
   4. Originality

D. **Personal Characteristics**
   1. Basic attitudes: likes and dislikes toward life, toward other characters in the play
   2. Ways of meeting a crisis, conflict, or change in environment
   3. Capacity for deep feeling
   4. Stability
   5. Self-control
   6. Temperament (genial, domineering, cowardly, and so on)

E. **Social Characteristics**
   1. Nationality
   2. Religion
   3. Social class
   4. Economic status
   5. Profession/daily routine

III. **Suggestions for Creation of Characters**

   A. Observe actual persons — real life! Note manner of walking; bodily attitude; certain gestures; facial expressions; tone and voice (find overall vocal pattern); characteristics and peculiarities in speech, dress, and so on

   B. Use symbols for suggesting human qualities
      1. Animals
      2. Machinery
      3. Objects

   C. Find one specific key image
      1. Recall own experiences and emotions
      2. Be inventive; use imagination. Explore — then select!

IV. **Analysis of Scene**

  A. Dramatic action or purpose of scene
     "What do I want in the scene?" (main objective)
     "What do I do to get what I want?" (the action)
     "What is in my way?" (the obstacle)

  B. What essence in the character will help him to get what he wants?

  C. What essence in the character will prevent him from getting it?

  D. Where is the climax or highest point of action?

BIBLIOGRAPHY AND RESOURCES

Background Studies

Bammel, Ernst, and C.F.D. Moule, eds. *Jesus and the Politics of His Day.* New York: Cambridge University Press, 1985.

Beers, V. Gilbert. *The Victor Handbook of Bible Knowledge.* Wheaton, Ill.: Victor Books, 1984.

Blaiklock, E.M. *The Archaeology of the New Testament.* Nashville: Thomas Nelson Publishers, 1984.

Bruce, F.F. *New Testament History.* New York: A Doubleday Anchor Book, 1972.

Coleman, William L. *Today's Handbook of Bible Times and Customs.* Minneapolis: Bethany House Publishers, 1984.

Edersheim, Alfred. *The History of the Jewish Nation* (3rd edition). Grand Rapids, Mich.: Baker, 1979.

Frank, Harry Thomas, ed. *Atlas of the Bible* (4th edition). New York: Reader's Digest, 1987.

Hoehner, Harold W. *Herod Antipas — A Contemporary of Jesus Christ.* Grand Rapids, Mich.: Zondervan Publishing House, 1980.

Jeremias, Joachim. *Jerusalem in the Time of Jesus* (3rd edition). Philadelphia: Fortress Press, 1978.

Maier, Paul L. *Pontius Pilate.* Wheaton, Ill.: Tyndale House, 1974.

Meeks, Wayne A. *The Moral World of the First Christians*. Philadelphia: The Westminster Press, 1986.

Jesus: His Life and Times. Old Tappan, N.J.: Revell Company, A Genesis Project Book, 1979.

Severy, Merle, ed. *Everyday Life in Bible Times* (4th century B.C.) Washington, D.C.: The National Geographic Society, 1968.

Weis, Dr. Pater Othmar. *Passion Oberammergau*. Aus der Furstenfeldbrucker 1811. Published by the community of Oberammergau, Germany, 1980.

Wright, G. Ernest, ed. *Great People of the Bible and How They Lived*. New York: Reader's Digest, 1979.

Storytelling/Theater Resources

Barrett, Ethel. *Storytelling — It's Easy!* Los Angeles: Cowman Publications, Inc. 1960.

Barton, Lucy. *Historic Costume for the Stage*. Boston: Walter Baker, 1935.

Bausch, William J. *Storytelling: Imagination and Faith*. Mystic, Conn.: Twenty-Third Publications, 1984.

Benedetti, Robert. *The Actor at Work*. Englewood Cliffs, N.J.: Prentice-Hall, 1970.

Blunt, Jerry. *Stage Dialects*. Scranton, Penn.: Chandler, 1966.

_____. *More Stage Dialects*. New York: Harper & Row, 1980.

_____. *The Composite Art of Acting*. New York: Macmillan, 1966.

Brockett, Oscar G. *The Theatre: An Introduction* (2nd edition). New York: Holt, Rinehart & Winston, 1969.

Brown, David M. *Dramatic Narrative in Preaching*. Valley Forge, Penn.: Judson Press, 1981.

Brown, Jeanette Perkins. *The Storyteller in Religious Education*. Boston: The Pilgrim Press, 1951.

Cather, Katherine Dunlap. *Story Telling for Teachers of Beginners and Primary Children*. New York: The Methodist Book Concern, 1921.

Chekhov, Michael. *The Actor*. New York: Harper, 1953.

Corson, Richard. *Stage Makeup* (7th edition). Englewood Cliffs, N.J.: Prentice-Hall, 1970.

Dean, Alexander, and Lawrence Carra. *Fundamentals of Play Directing* (revised edition). New York: Holt, Rinehart & Winston, 1965.

Friedrich, Willard, and John Frazer. *Scenery Design for the Amateur Stage*. New York: Macmillan, 1950.

Parker, W. Orin, and Harvey K. Smith. *Scene Design and Stage Lighting*. New York: Holt, Rinehart & Winston, 1963.

Rizzo, Raymond. *The Voice as an Instrument*. New York: Odyssey Press, 1969.

Royal, Claudia. *Storytelling*. Nashville: Broadman Press, 1955.

Spolin, Viola. *Improvisation for the Theater: A Handbook of Teaching and Directing Techniques*. Evanston, Ill.: Northwestern University Press, 1963.

Stanislavski, Constantin. *An Actor Prepares*. New York: Theatre Arts Books, 1936.

_____. *Building a Character*. New York: Theatre Arts Books, 1949.

St. John, Edward Porter. *Stories and Story-Telling in Moral and Religious Education*. New York: The Pilgrim Press, 1910.

Tanner, Fran Averett. *Basic Drama Projects*. Pocatello, Idaho: Clark Publishing Co, 1972.

Tooze, Ruth. *Storytelling*. Englewood Cliffs, N.J.: Prentice-Hall, 1959.

White, William R. *Speaking in Stories*. Minneapolis: Augsburg Publishing House, 1982.

Play Catalogues

Contemporary Drama Service, Box 7710-H3, Colorado Springs, Colorado 80933. Ask for catalogue of "Hard to Find Christian Participation Resources" and to be placed on the mailing list.

C.S.S. Publishing Company, 628 South Main Street, Lima, Ohio 45804. Ask for a catalogue of plays and to be placed on the mailing list.

Play Lists

Bristow, Eugene. *Directory of Long Plays for High Schools* (revised edition). National Thespian Society, 1961.

One Hundred Twenty Plays Recommended for Contest and Festival Use. American Educational Theatre Association, 1950. (Lists one-act and three-act plays.)

Plummer, Gail. *Dramatist's Guide to Selection of Plays and Musicals*. William Brown Co., 1963. (Lists plays for high school, college, community theater, children's theater. Also lists one-acts, classics, and musicals.)

Sievers, W. David. *Directing for the Theatre* (2nd edition). William Brown, 1965. (Appendix B lists one-act and three-act plays by number of characters.)

Dramatic Publishing Houses

Baker's Plays, 100 Chauncy Street, Boston, Massachusetts 02111.

The Costume Closet and Hansen Drama Shop, 718 East 3900 South, Salt Lake City, Utah 84107-2106. (801) 268-8466.

The Dramatic Publishing Company, 311 Washington (P.O. Box 109), Woodstock, Illinois 60098.

Dramatists Play Service, Inc., 440 Park Avenue South, New York, New York 10016.

I.E. Clark, Inc., Saint John's Road (P.O. Box 246), Schulenburg, Texas 78956-0246.

Lillenas Drama Newsletter, Lillenas Publishing Company, Box 419527, Kansas City, Missouri 64141.

Pioneer Drama Service, 2172 South Colorado Boulevard (Box 22555), Denver, Colorado 80222.

Reader's Theater Script Service, P.O. Box 178333, San Diego, California 92117. (619) 276-1948.

Samuel French, Inc., 25 West 45th Street, New York, New York 10036. (212) 382-0800. Ask for Basic Catalogue of Plays and for a Catalogue of Musicals.

Filmstrip Companies

Oleson Company, 1535 Ivar Avenue, Hollywood, California 90028. (Offers a series of 35mm filmstrips on scene construction, lighting, makeup, set design, and theater history.)

Makeup Houses

Bob Kelly Cosmetics, 151 West 46th Street, New York, New York 10036. (212) 819-0030.

Kryolan/Braendel GmbH, 1 Berlin 51, Papier-strasse 10, Federal Republic of Germany.

Leichner Makeup, Studio Imports, P.O. Box 143, South Pasadena, California 91030.

Max Factor Makeup Studios, 1666 North Highland Avenue, Los Angeles, California 90028. Or 1655 North McCadden Place, Hollywood, California 90028

Mehron, Inc., 150 West 46th Street, New York, New York 10036. (212) 524-1133. Or 325 West 37th Street, New York, New York 10018.

Nye, Ben, Inc., 11571 Santa Monica Boulevard, Los Angeles, California 90025. (213) 478-1558.

M. Stein Cosmetic Company, 430 Broome Street, New York, New York 10013.